The
MYSTERIOUS
SHROUD

The
MYSTERIOUS SHROUD

IAN WILSON

Photographs by
Vernon Miller

DOUBLEDAY & COMPANY, INC. · GARDEN CITY, NEW YORK
1986

Library of Congress Cataloging in Publication Data

Wilson, Ian, 1941–
The mysterious shroud.
Bibliography: p. 148
Includes index.
1. Holy Shroud.   I. Miller, Vernon.   II. Title.
BT587.S4W52   1986   232.9′66   83-45570
ISBN 0-385-19074-3

To Father Peter Rinaldi, S.D.B.,
whose inspiration has been infinite,
to mark his
Golden Jubilee

CONTENTS

ILLUSTRATIONS

COLOR

following page 14

The crowds at the Shroud exposition in Turin, Italy, 1978
Frontal aspect of human figure on Shroud, natural color
Dorsal aspect of human figure on Shroud, natural color
Face on the Shroud as it appears to the unaided eye, and in
  negative
VP8 Image Analyzer view of Shroud face
VP8 Image Analyzer view of frontal image on Shroud
The Shroud face in fluorescent light
Dr. Robert Bucklin, medical examiner for Los Angeles County

following page 46

STURP scientists smooth out wrinkles immediately prior to
  commencing their test program.
Frontal and dorsal views of the Shroud seen via transmitted
  light
Sam Pellicori examines the Shroud with a binocular
  microscope.
Photomicrograph of burn area on Shroud
Photomicrograph of body image area on Shroud, showing
  apparent absence of particulate matter
Photomicrograph of blood image area of Shroud, showing
  particulate matter
The Shroud illuminated for ultraviolet fluorescence
  photography during the 1978 testing
Close-up of body-image fibril showing "corroded" appearance
Close-up of nonbody-image fibril showing intact appearance
Photographer Vernon Miller records Doctors Jackson and
  Jumper examining the underside of the Shroud.

following page 110

Face of Christ, tenth century, S. Angelo in Formis, Capua, Italy
Face of Christ, fourth century, Hinton St. Mary, Dorset,
  England

BLACK AND WHITE

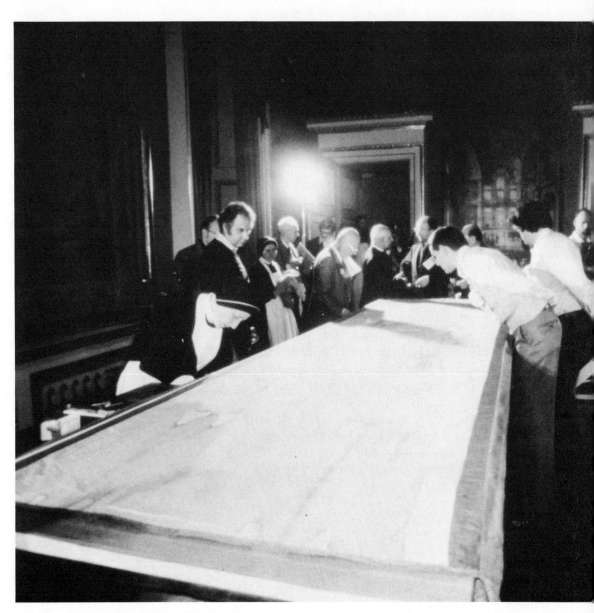

The night of October 8, 1978. In an ornate suite of the Royal Palace, Turin, nuns and scientists gather around the Shroud at the commencement of an intensive five days of scientific testing. To the left, nearest the camera, is one of the nuns who unstitched part of the Shroud's backing cloth to help in the examination of the underside. Nearly opposite is physicist Dr. John Jackson, one of the leaders of the U.S. Shroud of Turin Research Project. *(Barrie Schwortz)*

AUTHOR'S PREFACE

When my first book on the Shroud was published, in 1978, a scientific testing had been held five years before, a new testing was expected, and there were hopes of permission for a radiocarbon dating. As I write this, six years on, the current situation is almost identical.

Yet if it might seem that nothing of significance has happened during those years, nothing could be further from the truth. In October 1978, some two dozen U.S. scientists and technicians, accompanied by some eight thousand pounds of specialist equipment, spent one hundred twenty working hours in Turin conducting the most exhaustive tests to which any religious object has ever been submitted. In the years that have followed, their often highly technical reports have appeared in dozens of well-respected journals: "Physics and Chemistry of the Shroud of Turin," in *Analytica Chimica Acta;* "Ultraviolet fluorescence photography of the Shroud of Turin," in the *Journal of Biological Photography;* "Blood on the Shroud of Turin," in *Applied Optics;* and many more. The layman might expect that such high-powered investigations would at least have succeeded in establishing whether the Shroud is a genuine burial wrapping or a forgery; yet, if anything, these issues have become even more confused.

According to the internationally respected microanalyst Dr. Walter McCrone, former magician Joe Nickell, and a variety of contributors to *The Skeptical Inquirer,* the Shroud is the work of an artist. This contention is claimed as proved by the presence of artists' pigments among samples taken from the Shroud's surface in 1978, corroborated by medieval documents indicating that an artist created the cloth's "imprint" image in the mid-fourteenth century. Yet, according to the overwhelming majority of those scientists who worked directly on the Shroud in 1978, McCrone and Nickell are wrong. They contend that the true Shroud image is demonstrably of natural formation (albeit not fully understood) and that the pigments are readily explicable as incidental debris. Recent popular books have served only to accentuate this polarization of attitudes. The Reverend David Sox, earlier favorable to the Shroud's authenticity, underwent a mind-blowingly rapid conversion in order to become McCrone's mouthpiece with *The Image on the Shroud*, published in 1981. Conversely, a far too rose-tinted view of the 1978 testing was offered by Kenneth Stevenson and Gary Habermas' *Verdict on the Shroud*, published in the same year. Two years later, Joe Nickell's overly dismissive *Inquest on the Shroud of Turin* was followed by Frank Tribbe's overly credulous *Portrait of Jesus?* and Dr. John Heller's *Report on the Shroud of Turin*. The latter, although refreshingly free of such faults, has presented recent Shroud scientific work in an amusing but so fictionalized way that the discerning reader may be at somewhat of a loss to know what to accept as fact.

In my first book, I made clear my personal belief in the Shroud's authenticity, a belief I have continued to hold despite having the highest regard for Dr. Walter McCrone, whose involvement in the subject was directly at my instigation. Until recently, my stance has been the somewhat awkward one of not believing McCrone to be right, yet, as a nonscientist, having insufficient grasp of the scientific complexities to be able to understand how he could be wrong.

Now, however, I believe that there has been sufficiently meaningful publication of the 1978 scientific work for an altogether more confident presentation of this than hitherto, and it is this aim that underlies the present book. Cognizant of the need for a sensible middle voice between the too polarized attitudes of other authors, I have tried to be fair to all shades of opinion on the Shroud. The reader who favors the Shroud's being the work of an artist will not, I trust, find a fudging of the case for this in Chapter 5. Conversely, the reader who has felt the need for pro-authenticity scientific reports to be translated into laymen's language should, I hope, find that need met in Chapter 6. For readers hitherto unfamiliar with previous books on the Shroud, in the first three chapters I have summarized background information to be found in more detail in my earlier *The Shroud of Turin* (Doubleday, 1978). But even those fully conversant with the subject should find delight in one long-overdue feature: the plethora of high-quality photographs, which so many previous books have lacked. Both the quality and the quantity of these are due largely to the efforts of my photographic coauthor, Vernon Miller, who as a member of STURP (the U.S. Shroud of Turin Research Project) was directly responsible for photographing much of the 1978 scientific testing.

If Vern Miller's photographs add a visual grace to this book, responsible for grace of a quite different kind has been Salesian

Father Peter Rinaldi, whose quiet work furthering interest in the Shroud is now a fifty-year-old legend. It was in 1935, two years after seeing the Shroud for himself in Turin, that the newly ordained Rinaldi crossed the Atlantic to become much-loved pastor of Corpus Christi Church, Port Chester, New York. There, taking up the Shroud as what he calls his "spiritual hobby," he penned articles and books on the subject and created within the church an exquisitely tasteful Shroud shrine. It was before this shrine that, while still an agnostic, I knelt with Father Rinaldi on my first-ever visit to New York, in 1971. And it was almost entirely through his patient diplomatic negotiations with Turin's ecclesiastical authorities and the cloth's then formal owner, the late Umberto II of Savoy, that the so extensive U.S. involvement in the 1978 testing was permitted. The year 1985 marks Father Rinaldi's Golden Jubilee as a priest, and this book is unhesitatingly dedicated to him to mark those fifty years of spiritual inspiration and achievement.

I am also grateful to the following for information and advice in the course of the preparation of this book: Dr. Alan Adler, biochemist, Western Connecticut State University; Dr. William Airth-Kindree, medical specialist, Urbana, Illinois; Dr. Geoffrey Allen, professor of chemistry, Berkeley Nuclear Laboratories, Berkeley, Gloucestershire, England; Dr. Robert Bucklin, deputy medical examiner, Los Angeles County; Professor Werner Bulst, S.J., New Testament scholar, Technical University of Darmstadt, West Germany; Professor Averil Cameron, historian, Kings College, London University, England; Professor James Cameron, Home Office pathologist, the London Hospital Medical School, England; Dr. Robin Cormack, art specialist, Courtauld Institute of Art, England; Mrs. Dorothy Crispino, editor, *Shroud Spectrum*, Nashville, Indiana; Dr. Eugene Csocsán de Várallja, demographer and historian, Oxford University, England; Noel Currer-Briggs, genealogist, Cambridge, England; the late Reverend Francis Filas, S.J., professor of theology, Loyola University, Chicago; Don Luigi Fossati, S.D.B., theological scholar, Scuolo Professionale Salesiano, Turin, Italy; Peter Freeland, head of science, Worth School, England; the late Dr. Max Frei, former director, the Police Scientific Laboratory, Zurich, Switzerland; Professor Luigi Gonella, physicist, Turin University, Italy; Professor Edward Hall, director, Oxford University Research Laboratory for Archaeology and the History of Art, England; Dr. John Jackson, research professor, physics, University of Colorado; Maria Jepps, translator, Wells, England; Dr. Walter McCrone, microanalyst, McCrone Research Institute, Chicago; Paul Maloney, director, Ancient Near

Eastern Researches, Quakertown, Pennsylvania; Dr. Allan Mills, geophysicist, Leicester University, England; Robert Mottern, radiographer, Sandia Laboratories, Albuquerque; Rev. Adam Otterbein, president, Holy Shroud Guild, Esopus, New York; Samuel Pellicori, optical physicist, Santa Barbara Research Center, California; John Ray, reader in Egyptology, Cambridge University, England; Giovanni Riggi, microanalyst, Società Progettazione Riggi, Turin, Italy; Barrie Schwortz, photographer, Santa Barbara, California; Dr. Les Strong, entomologist, Bristol University, England; Victor Tunkel, Jewish scholar, Faculty of Laws, Queen Mary College, London, England; John Tyrer, textile specialist, Manchester, England; Dr. Jean Volckringer, retired chemist, Paris, France; Dr. Alan Whanger, psychiatrist and researcher in Shroud iconography, Durham, North Carolina; Dr. Lucas Wüthrich, curator of sculpture, Schwizerisches Landesmuseum, Zurich, Switzerland; Dr. Frederick Zugibe, chief medical examiner, Rockland County, New York.

I am also grateful to Doubleday editor Robert Heller and assistant Theresa D'Orsogna for their quiet patience and encouragement during the years this book has been in preparation, and for choosing a particularly pertinent moment to steer the book to publication.

Bristol
England

IAN WILSON
April 1985

The
MYSTERIOUS
SHROUD

The Shroud as understood in the sixteenth century, from an aquatint attributed to the Italian artist Giovanni Battista della Rovere. In the upper portion of the picture is Della Rovere's depiction of the Shroud, inclusive of the 1532 fire damage. Below is the artist's suggestion of how the body was originally laid in the cloth to create the strange head-to-head images. (*Galleria Sabauda, Scala/EPA Inc.*)

1

THE MYSTERY OF THE SHROUD

It was late August 1978. As, in Rome, the conclave of cardinals sat in the Sistine Chapel in the final stages of choosing a successor to Pope Paul VI, three hundred miles to the north in a chapel in the Piedmontese city of Turin, another, much smaller group of clergy were in the throes of an almost equally auspicious undertaking. In the Royal Chapel, set high to the rear of Turin's Cathedral of St. John the Baptist, the group watched attentively as one of their number precariously ascended a small ladder set against the black marble of the chapel's central altar. At the top of the steps, the priest cautiously unlocked two metal grilles, then began to bring down a long wooden box. Opened, this revealed an ornate silver casket, which in its turn disclosed a cylindrical bundle wrapped in red silk. Gently laid on a long table, the bundle began to be unrolled, revealing a surprising length of patched, stained linen which all present studied with an extraordinary intentness before proceeding to their appointed tasks.

A few hours later, at 11 P.M. on Saturday, August 26, that same length of linen hung thumbtacked to a wooden board inside an illuminated, bullet-proof-glass case suspended just in front of the Cathedral's main altar. There came to gaze first representatives of the world's press, then worshipers at a special inaugural Mass, then, almost simultaneously with the announcement of the election of Pope John Paul I, the first of what would be more than three million pilgrims from almost every country in the world. For the first time in forty-five years, the Holy Shroud of Turin—reputedly the very cloth in which Jesus Christ was wrapped in the tomb two thousand years ago—was on public display. During the next six weeks, pilgrims would shuffle past the display case at the rate of seventy-five thousand per day, each one conscious that this might be his or her only opportunity for another generation. For each of these, just as for those who, around the world, viewed the same object on their television screens, there could only be one overriding question. Was this really Jesus' very burial wrapping, incredibly preserved through nearly two thousand years, or

1

was it, like so many other Christian relics, simply another cynical forgery?

As becomes obvious to anyone who seriously studies the Shroud, the question admits no easy answer. If the Shroud and what it bears is the work of some forger or hoaxer, it is not by one who skimped his task. The physical length sprawls a generous four and a half meters, with a width of one and one tenth meters. Eight centimeters from one edge, a mysterious seam runs the full length of the cloth, apparently joining-on a strip of the same fabric. From this strip, a pocket-handkerchief-size piece appears missing at each end.

The fabric, in a fine, tightly woven herringbone twill, is in surprisingly good condition, soft and pliable, and just a little heavier than shirt cloth. Although it shows little sign of wear or disintegration, very readily apparent are marks of a known damage incident. This is reliably documented to have occurred the night of December 4, 1532, as the Shroud lay in a silver casket locked behind a grille set into the wall of the beautiful Sainte-Chapelle at Chambéry, today in eastern France. What was most likely an accidentally overturned candle caused a fire to spread rapidly among the chapel's rich hangings. Although would-be rescuers were quickly on the scene, they realized that the keys to the grille lay in the hands of various dignitaries whom it would be impossible to summon in time. Fortunately someone had the presence of mind to summon the local blacksmith, and the Shroud's preservation to this day owes much to this unknown man's courage, strength, and skill.

By the time he managed to prize open the grille, the heat was so intense that the Shroud's silver casket had already begun to melt. When this was opened up, a drop of molten silver was found to have fallen on one edge of the Shroud's folds, needing a swift drenching in water before the flames sputtered out. The damage sustained that night consisted of two long lines of holes and scorches, having a patterned appearance deriving from the forty-eight layers in which the Shroud had been folded. Patches sewn on in 1534 by a team of Poor Clare nuns serve to disguise the worst of this damage, and the linen was strengthened at the same time by the sewing on of a holland-cloth backing sheet. Even the water used for the dousing can be seen to have left its mark in the form of several lozenge-shaped stains to be found centrally at intervals along the length of the cloth, with mirror images of each along the sides.

The 1532 occasion was not, in fact, the only incident in which the Shroud has been touched by fire. A painting of 1516 shows

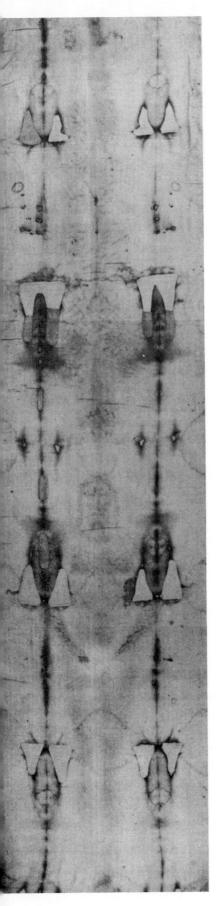

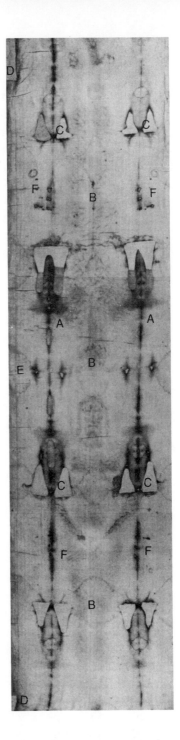

The Shroud as it looks today, approximately 14½ feet long by 3½ feet wide. Obvious at first glance is the damage caused in 1532: two long lines of scorches (A), lozenge-shaped stains caused by water used to quench the fire (B), and patches sewn on by Poor Clare nuns (C). Portions appear to have been removed (D) at each end of a long seam line (E), and four sets of triple holes (F) can only derive from some damage prior to 1532, since they occur in a painting of 1516. Between the scorch lines is the mysterious, shadowy imprint of the back and front of a human figure. (Vernon Miller)

four sets of holes in the Shroud, each set comprising three main holes with peripheral surrounding damage (see page 79). These holes are still identifiable, and reconstruction of their original arrangement suggests that at one stage the cloth was folded in four and deliberately run through three times with something like a red-hot poker. Exactly why and when someone inflicted such damage has gone unrecorded.

Undoubtedly the Shroud's most fascinating feature, however, lies between the fire marks, in the form of what appear to be impressions of the back and front of a full-size human figure (color plates 2 and 3). The color of the impressions is a uniform sepia, or yellow-brown, very shadowy in character, with, particularly unmistakably, a mask-like bearded face with seemingly owlish, staring eyes and skeletal-looking hands crossed over the loins. The obvious theory behind the imprints is that a body was laid on one half of the linen, the other half of the cloth being drawn over the head and down to the feet, thus creating two head-to-head images. A gap between the front- and the back-of-the-body images corresponds with what would have been the top of the head. Parts of the body that would have been farthest from contact with the cloth, such as the fronts of the shoulders and the backs of the knees appropriately fail to register. As another convincing-looking touch, the front of the body image stops short at the ankles, suggesting that not quite enough length was allowed for this half of the cloth to cover the feet (or that a portion was cut off). Conveying the idea that this was a victim of crucifixion are intricate, carmine-colored splashes resembling bloodstains at the arms, feet, and chest and across the small of the back.

The whole effect is eerie, ephemeral. Only at a distance do the images make some sort of sense. Viewed in close-up, the body features become incomprehensible, because of their faintness seeming to disappear into the cloth. Seen under a magnifying glass, the image areas appear totally lacking in substance such as paint or pigments. To the whole there is not the slightest semblance of an artist's style of any historical period.

Of extraordinary interest, therefore, is what happens to the Shroud's image when it is reversed by black-and-white photography into a photographic negative (pages 6–9). The now famous discovery associated with this took place in the year 1898, at the time of one of the rare expositions, when a prominent Turin councillor, Secondo Pia, was asked to make the first-ever official photograph of the Shroud. Photography was still a relatively new science at this time, and for Pia the assignment presented some

Above: Pilgrim's medallion of the Shroud exhibited at Lirey, ca. 1357. The first known representation of the Shroud entirely full length, i.e., with both frontal and dorsal images visible. The shields are the arms of Geoffrey de Charny on the left and his second wife and subsequent widow, Jeanne de Vergy, on the right. The roundel in the center represents the Empty Tomb. From a damaged amulet found in the Seine by the Pont au Change and now in the Musée de Cluny, Paris. *(Ref. 75 CN 5261, Service de documentation photographique de la Réunion des musées nationaux)*

Right: The casket in which the Shroud, wrapped in red silk, is stored. *(Dr. David Willis)*

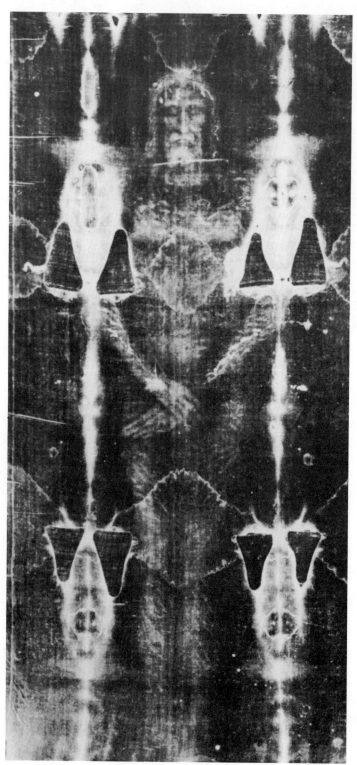

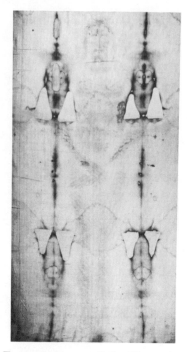

Frontal aspect of the Shroud as it appears in negative, and (inset above) to the unaided eye. Note how the negative photographically reveals natural light and shade. What appear to be bloodstains along the arms, in the chest, and on the forehead show up in white. *(Vernon Miller)*

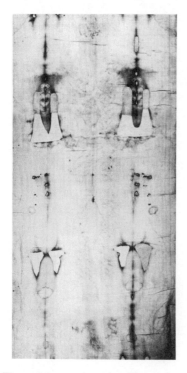

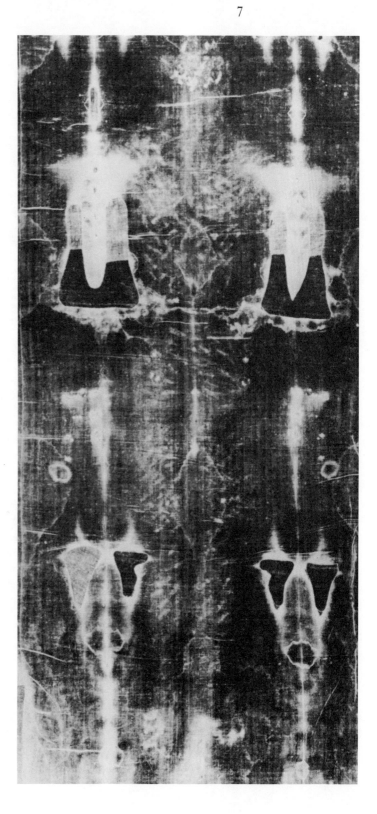

Dorsal image on the Shroud as it appears in negative, and (inset above) to the unaided eye. *(Vernon Miller)*

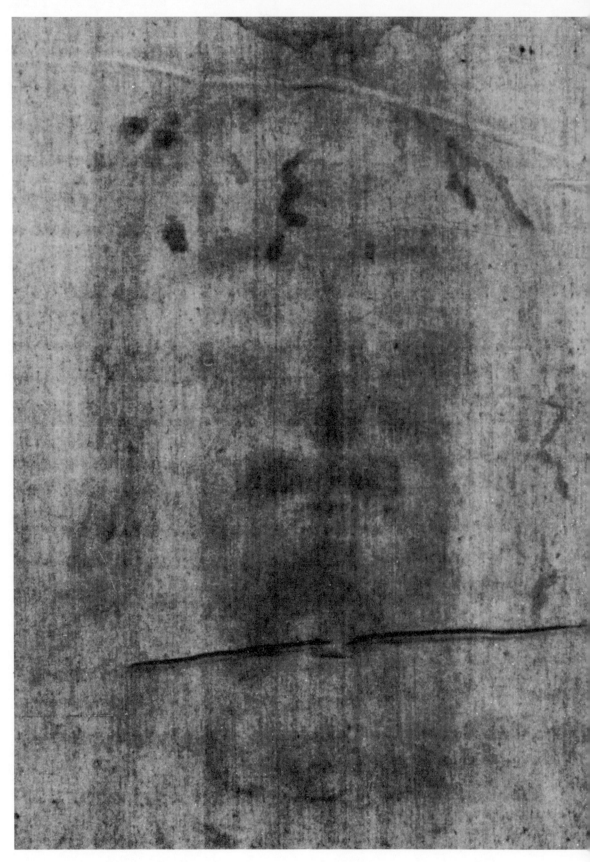

Face on the Shroud as it appears to the unaided eye. *(Vernon Miller)*

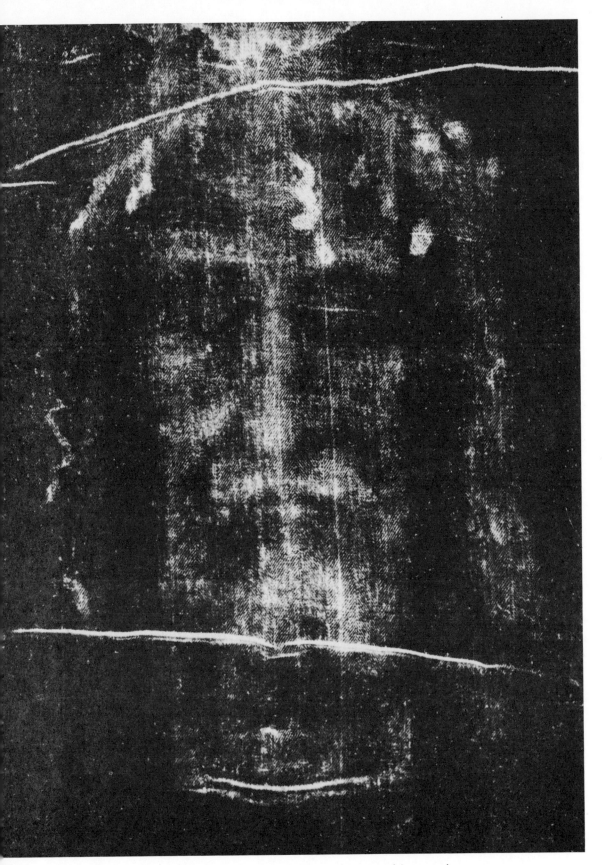

Face on the Shroud as it appears on a photographic negative.
(British Society for the Turin Shroud)

special difficulties. Because of the crowds of pilgrims viewing the Shroud in the daytime, he could work only at night, when the Cathedral was closed. This meant the use of electric lighting, new and somewhat uncertain at that time. He also had to build a special platform so that his camera could be at the same height as the Shroud's display case. After an abortive attempt on May 25, the night of May 28, Pia successfully took two exposures on large glass negative plates customary for the photography of the time, then hurried back to his darkroom to develop them.

Because of the already shadowy and ghostlike nature of the Shroud image, Pia expected that anything he had managed to capture on the photographic negative plate, itself invariably a ghost of the original, would be even more difficult to distinguish. Nothing, therefore, prepared him for the shock that awaited him that night. As under the developer recognizable features of the Shroud began to appear, the cloth now black, the dark scorch marks from the 1532 fire showing up white, he observed an extraordinary change in the Shroud's double-figure image. For the first time visible in natural relief, with lifelike highlights and shadows as on a real photograph, the body could be seen to be well-proportioned and of an impressive build. The apparent bloodstains, showing up white, similarly took on a striking realism as injuries to the hands, feet, chest, and crown of the head. Instead of the owlish, mask-like face, the photographic negative revealed a hauntingly majestic countenance, with eyes closed in death (color plates 4 and 5). As Pia came to believe that moment and for the rest of his life, the image on the negative must be the actual appearance of the body of Christ when laid in the tomb. Somehow the Shroud itself was a kind of photographic negative, which became positive when reversed by the camera.

Whatever the validity of such an interpretation, incontrovertibly Pia's discovery was no nineteenth-century hoax or once-in-a-lifetime freak. In 1931, Italian professional photographer Giuseppe Enrie took a new and far more definitive set of photographs, including details of the face and close-ups of the bloodstains. In 1969 and 1973, more photographs were taken, and in 1978 literally millions of visitors to the expositions of that year were freely allowed to use their cameras. Every technical advance in black-and-white photography has revealed the negative characteristics in greater clarity.

The question that obviously arises is whether any forger, centuries before the age of photography, could *really* have managed to create such an extraordinary image, working in negative, yet without any means of checking his work. It is clearly important for us to try to learn more about exactly how this cloth has come down to us, and in particular how far with certainty it can be traced back through history.

For at least a provisional answer to this, the clock needs to be turned back almost six centuries, to the French city of Troyes in the autumn of the year 1389. From there the bishop of the time, Pierre d'Arcis, a former lawyer, sent a strongly worded complaint to his Pope, Clement VII, in Avignon. As D'Arcis explained, he wished to draw the Pope's attention to a scandal which he had uncovered in the tiny collegiate church of Lirey, twelve miles from Troyes, and within his diocese. To his extreme displeasure the church's canons had:

> falsely and deceitfully, being consumed with the passion of avarice and not from any motive of devotion but only of gain, procured for their church a certain cloth cunningly painted, upon which by clever sleight of hand was depicted the twofold image of one man, that is to say the back and front, they falsely declaring and pretending that this was the actual Shroud in which our Saviour Jesus Christ was enfolded in the tomb.

With regard to how the cloth had been procured, D'Arcis said he had found out that it had first been exhibited in Lirey some thirty years earlier, at the time of one of his predecessors, Bishop Henry of Poitiers. When the matter was brought to his attention, Bishop Henry made inquiries and

> . . . discovered the fraud and how the said cloth had been cunningly painted, the truth being attested by the artist who had painted it, to wit, that it was a work of human skill, and not miraculously wrought or bestowed.

As D'Arcis emphasized to the Pope:

> . . . this could not be the real Shroud of Our Lord having the Saviour's likeness thus imprinted upon it, since the holy Gospel made no mention of any such imprint, while if it had been true it was quite unlikely that the holy Evangelists would have omitted to record it, or that the fact should have remained hidden until the present time.

Historically there can appear nothing but sound sense to D'Arcis' information and observations. Before the Lirey affair, there is indeed no clear record of the existence of any figure-imprinted shroud of Jesus. When the Pia revelations first came to light, at the end of the nineteenth century, all possible surviving sources were very thoroughly searched by Catholic historians Canon Ulysse Chevalier of France and Rev. Herbert Thurston of England. With the minor exception of a mysterious figure-imprinted *sydoine* mentioned by a crusader in Constantinople in 1203, all early references to preserved shrouds of Jesus make no mention of any (all-important) imprint, and can generally be traced to other, rival relics.

Nor can there be much doubt that the "cunningly painted" cloth of Lirey which so offended Bishop d'Arcis and his predecessor is one and the same as the cloth known today as the Turin Shroud. The family who owned the church and the cloth in Lirey were the De Charnys, the most prominent member being Geoffrey de Charny, who founded the Lirey church in 1353 and was killed at the battle of Poitiers three years later. In the nineteenth century was found in the Seine a fourteenth-century pilgrim's amulet which, although damaged, shows an exposition of what certainly looks like the present-day Shroud. Also clearly visible on the amulet are shields with the arms of Geoffrey de Charny and his wife, Jeanne de Vergy, flanking a roundel showing Christ's empty tomb.

The justice of Bishop d'Arcis' arguments is further reinforced by documents of Geoffrey de Charny's son (contemporary with D'Arcis and whom we will refer to as Geoffrey II), which consistently refer to the relic not as the real burial cloth of Jesus, but only as a "likeness or representation," a formula repeated by Geoffrey II's daughter, Margaret de Charny, and her husband Humbert de Villersexel, who, in the early-fifteenth century, kept the Shroud at St. Hippolyte sur Doubs.

It was this Margaret who, in 1453, by then widowed and childless, ceded the Shroud to Duke Louis of Savoy, in the hands of whose descendants the Shroud had been preserved ever since, until willed to the Vatican upon the death of Umberto of Savoy in 1983. Intriguingly, only with this change to more illustrious ownership did the Shroud begin to lose its fraudulent associations, and with remarkable rapidity. As early as 1464 the future Pope Sixtus IV, Francesco della Rovere, wrote of it as "coloured with the blood of Christ." Just over forty years later, Sixtus' nephew, Pope Julius II, gave the cloth a special feast day as *the* Holy Shroud (although not the only recognized holy shroud). By 1578, the relic was the Savoy family's sacred palladium, moved with great ceremony to their new capital of Turin, where it has been ever since. Today, while the Catholic Church does not demand belief in the Shroud's authenticity, or that of any other relic, few would take any other claimant seriously.

The Shroud, then, presents an extraordinary enigma. Ostensibly it *ought* to be a forgery. After all, it seems a far-fetched idea that a piece of linen of such a size should have survived nearly two thousand years (even though there are surviving Egyptian burial linens twice as old). It seems equally far-fetched that in the case of none other than Jesus Christ a photographic image should have been left on the cloth. If it is a natural phenomenon, why are there no other surviving examples? The D'Arcis accusations of forgery seem authoritative and sound, and derive from a time when, undeniably, forgery of religious relics was rife. Above all, there is the very damning historical silence before the fourteenth century. If genuine, the Shroud *must* have been around somewhere during those earlier centuries, and it seems extremely unlikely that extant documentary sources are too incomplete to contain a record of it.

Yet if we seriously try to think of the Shroud as a forgery, we similarly come across some powerful objections. How could any artist, either by accident or design, have produced an image so convincingly photographic when seen in negative, five hundred years before the opportunity existed to check his work, and for anyone else to appreciate it properly? Why should he want to do so, when no one of his own time would have been able to appreciate his cleverness? Significantly, artists' copies of the Shroud, made in later periods artistically far more competent than the fourteenth century, look crude and almost ludicrously amateur by comparison to their original.

Furthermore, in order to produce the Shroud's negativity, an artist of any period would have needed to discipline himself to work consistently in the very reverse of the light-and-shade modeling principles by which he would have been trained. This is extremely difficult, as attested by modern artists who have tried making exact replicas of the Shroud, among these Britain's John Weston, an agnostic commissioned to produce a duplicate Shroud for the television documentary *The Silent Witness* in 1978, and an artist from Manchester who undertook simply to copy the Shroud face for the BBC television QED program on the Shroud shown in November 1982.

Yet even if it is argued that the Shroud shows the genuine imprint of a human body, either Jesus or, as has been seriously suggested, someone crucified in the fourteenth century for forgery purposes, the problems are little less complex. Although the Shroud's image might appear to be what one would expect from contact with a bloodstained, sweat-soaked body, in practice a body would produce an image only where there was direct contact, and no image where there was not. Whether a forgery or the result of a natural process, the Shroud's delicate inverse shadings cannot have been produced by an ordinary contact imprinting method. All attempts at replicating such printings invariably prove unsatisfactory and distorted because of the human body's three-dimensionality.

Then there is the appearance of the Shroud's blood flows. Logically one would expect nothing more than a mess from the adhesion of a linen cloth 'to a bloodstained body. For instance, if the chronology of Jesus' crucifixion is followed, we would anticipate only a little imprint from early injuries, such as the crowning with thorns, the blood from which would have dried early in the day, while late injuries, such as the wound in the side, would be expected to show up very clearly. Irrationally, on the Shroud all apparent bloodstains appear with the same completeness and clarity irrespective of their theoretical time of origin. And they are far more reddish and fresh-looking than would seem right for blood that theoretically dried on the cloth nearly two thousand years ago.

The Shroud is, then, an object of genuine mystery, and one for which, despite the most intensive recent efforts, there exists no entirely satisfactory explanation, whatever viewpoint is adopted. The challenge it presents is that it is not a Bermuda triangle or Von Däniken-type mystery. It exists. It has been made freely accessible to international scientific investigation, as was allowed to a team of no less than twenty-four U.S. scientists in 1978. It ought not to be beyond the resources of twentieth-century science at least to determine whether it is a painting or a genuine gravecloth. Yet as will become obvious, reaching even so ostensibly preliminary a finding is by no means as simple as it might at first appear . . .

1. The crowds at the cathedral in Turin, Italy, for the exposition of the Shroud in 1978. *(Barrie M. Schwortz)*

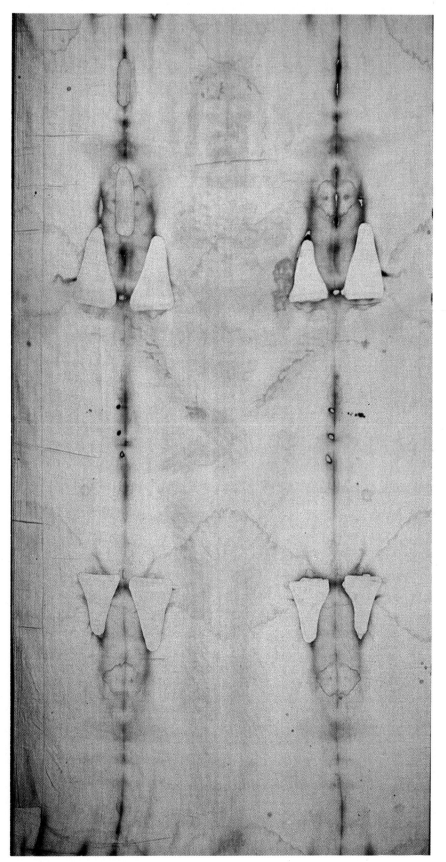

2. Frontal aspect of human figure on the Shroud, natural color.
(Vernon Miller)

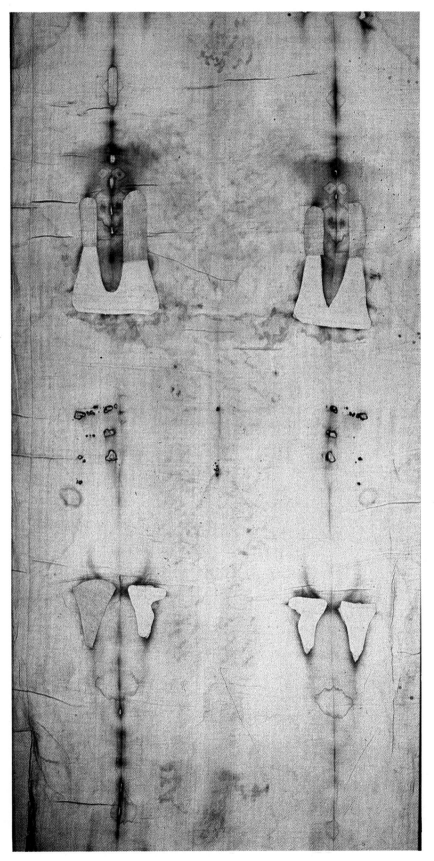

3. Dorsal aspect of human figure on the Shroud, natural color.
(Vernon Miller)

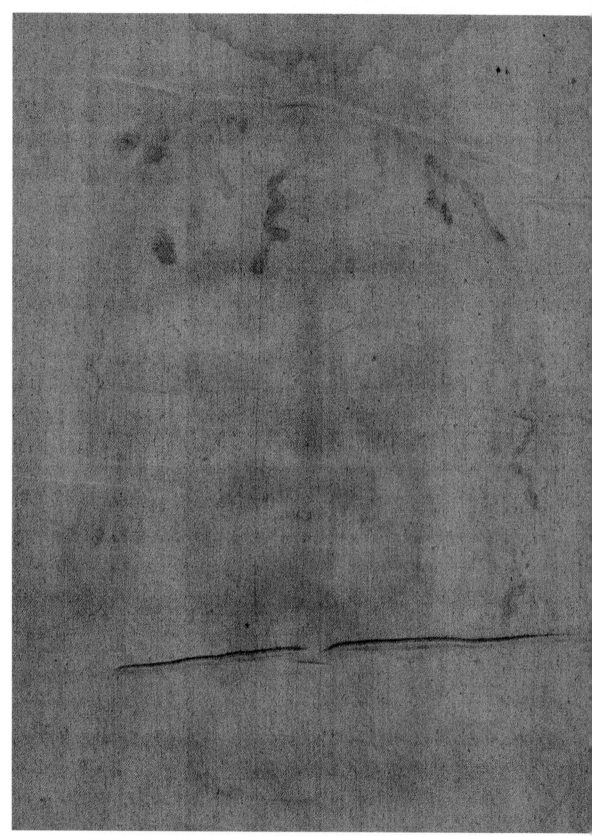

4. Face on the Shroud as it appears to the unaided eye, natural color. *(Vernon Miller)*

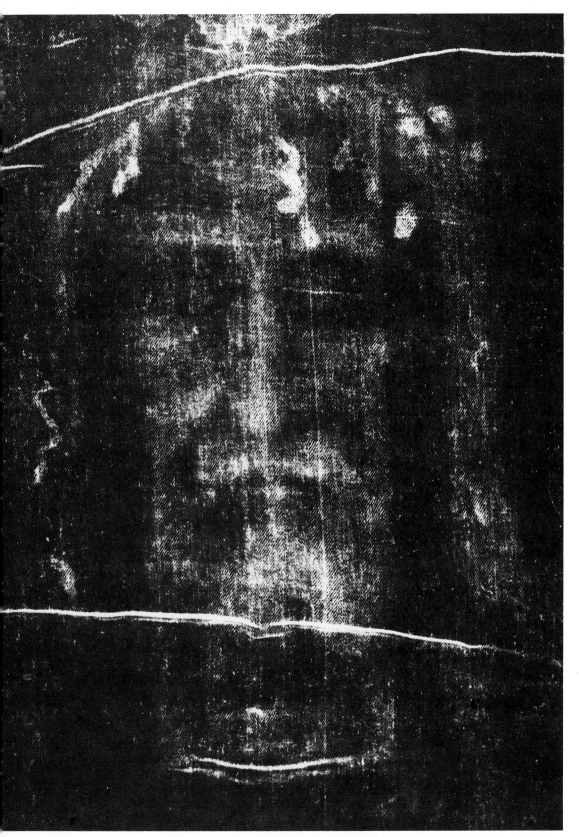

5. Face on the Shroud as it appears on a photographic negative.
(*British Society for the Turin Shroud*)

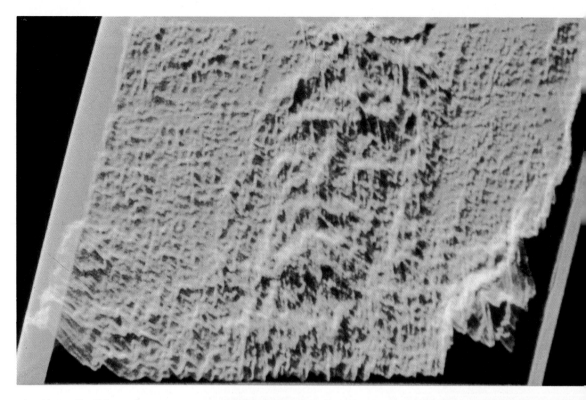

6. *Above:* Striking, three-dimensional view of the Shroud face, as revealed on the NASA program's VP8 Image Analyzer. *(Vernon Miller)*

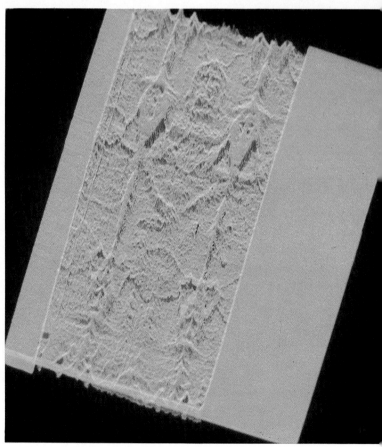

7. *Right:* The Shroud frontal image seen three-dimensionally, as revealed by the VP8 Image Analyzer. *(Vernon Miller)*

8. The Shroud face, as seen in flourescent light. *(Vernon Miller)*

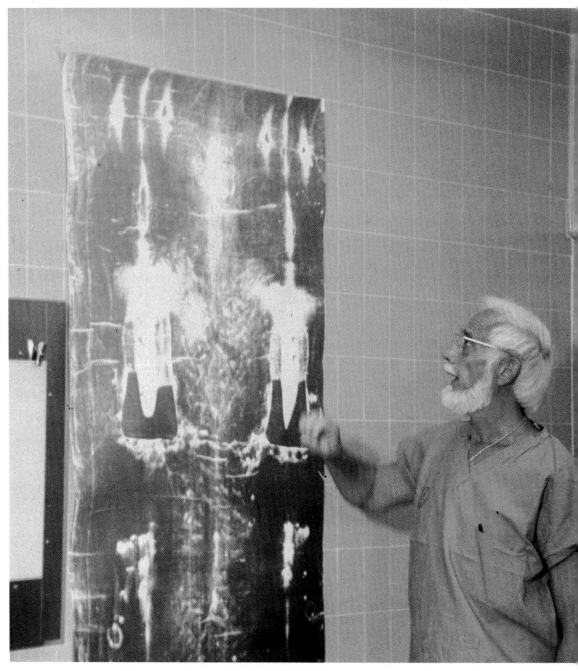

9. U.S. pathologist Dr. Robert Bucklin, medical examiner for Los Angeles County, California, reviews Shroud negative as a medically convincing photograph of a crucifixion victim. Many forensic specialists across the world share Dr. Bucklin's opinion. *(Screenpro)*

2

THE SHROUD AND
THE PATHOLOGIST

When in the year 1607 English scholars were working on the
King James, or Authorised, Version of the Bible, they translated
one of St. Paul's references to his earthly view of Jesus with the
words "through a glass darkly."

A strikingly evocative phrase, it had extraordinary appropriate-
ness to the subtle, black-backgrounded image of a crucified man
seen on the Shroud photographic negative. Some see this as so
obviously photographic that doubts seem superfluous. Skeptics in
all honesty do not see it this way. Even among upholders of authenticity, quite different images of the body may be formed in
different minds, some seeing a tightly drawn-in stomach, others a
potbelly, some seeing genitals, others denying this. There is
clearly an elusive quality to the Shroud, as impenetrable to the
enthusiast as it is unappealing to the skeptic.

Nevertheless, while to date no recognized art scholar has come
forward conclusively to identify the Shroud image with a specific
artist or period of art, many reputable scientific individuals, by no
means all Christians, have been prepared to accept the same image as a proper documentary photograph and to make deductions
about what it shows. It is these deductions, independent of examination of the cloth itself, which formed almost the entire basis for
Shroud research up to the year 1978.

As generally agreed by most observers, the visible body on the
Shroud appears to be that of a thirty-to-forty-five-year-old male,
quite naked, with beard and mustache and hair falling to the
shoulders. At the back of the head seems to be visible a long, loose
rope of hair extending down the spine to the level of the shoulder
blades. Although anthropological deductions are inevitably subjective, ethnologist Carleton S. Coon has associated the man with
the very pure Semitic type found today among noble Arabs and
Sephardic Jews, and certainly there are at least broad hints of
Jewishness in the hair styling. The seemingly unbound rope of

15

hair at the back of the head accords with what German biblical scholar H. Gressman has referred to as one of the commonest fashions for Jewish men in antiquity, to which French scriptural authority Daniel-Rops has supportively added the information that the Jews normally wore this "plaited and rolled up under their headgear" except on public holidays.

Estimates of the man's height have varied, mainly because of differences of interpretation concerning the exact lie of the cloth over the body, but there would seem little doubt that he was tall. The original maximum estimated height was around 180 centimeters (5 foot 10 1/2 inches), but more recent researchers have scaled this down to around 170 centimeters (5 foot 7 inches). Even this latter figure has been challenged from the viewpoint that it is too tall for the average man of two thousand years ago, but this at least is an argument easy to dispose of. That people of antiquity were significantly shorter than ourselves is one of the most widespread popular fallacies, as has been conclusively demonstrated by a University of California special investigation. Skeletons of ten adult males from a recently discovered first-century Jewish burial ground in Jerusalem included one even of the upper height estimate of the man of the Shroud, and there is no reason to believe 170 centimeters would be any more exceptional in Jesus' time than today.

Obviously a major preliminary consideration from the point of view of the possible authenticity of the Shroud is whether a human body would actually fit the parameters the cloth's imprints indicate, and this is an issue similarly easy to resolve. A research program on this very question was undertaken by two U.S. Air Force assistant professors, Drs. Jackson and Jumper, leaders of the 1978 U.S. Shroud testing team. Using a full-size muslin replica of the Shroud, they marked out on this all the salient body features and then among friends and associates recruited volunteers to fit the markings. Using individuals of appropriate height and weight (around 165 to 180 pounds), they not only found convincing physical correspondence, they were also able closely to reconstruct the hypothetical body's burial attitude. It had, for instance, to have been set at a slight angle, the head raised by some pillow-type support, the arms drawn very stiffly over the pelvis, the right shoulder set lower than the left, the legs decisively flexed at the knees, and the left foot partly over the right. If the Shroud is a forgery, the care with which even the postcrucifixion lie of the body has been thought out is quite remarkable.

But perhaps the most compelling aspect of the Shroud as a subject of inquiry is the extent to which the visible blood flows

and physical injuries have been viewed as authentic by members
of the medical profession. As early as April 21, 1902, and therefore within four years of the announcement of Pia's photographic
revelations, Yves Delage, professor of anatomy at the Paris Sor-
bonne, gave a lecture to the French Académie des Sciences in
which he claimed that the Shroud body image and wounds are
physiologically so flawless and meaningful that he found it impossible to believe they could be the work of an artist. To the scandal
of his rationalist colleagues, who had always known him as an
agnostic, Delage said he found no difficulty in believing that the
body wrapped in the Shroud was that of Jesus.

When, in 1931, Giuseppe Enrie's photographs revealed the
Shroud image in yet greater clarity, into Delage's shoes stepped
Dr. Pierre Barbet, chief surgeon at St. Joseph's Hospital, Paris.
Fascinated by some of the thitherto unexpected features of crucifixion the Shroud seemed to indicate, Barbet began remarkable
experiments on cadavers, subsequently publishing a very supportive book on the Shroud's authenticity under the title *A Doctor
at Calvary*. Since Barbet, such medical support has grown year by
year. A decade ago, the leading figures were Milan forensic medicine professor Giovanni Judica-Cordiglia, New York physician
Dr. Anthony Sava, and British general practitioner Dr. David
Willis, who died in 1976. Today the scene includes, among many
others, British Home Office pathologist Professor James Cameron
of the London Hospital, famous for his association with the Australian Ayers Rock child murder case; Australian anatomy professor Dr. Michael Blunt of the University of Sydney, Australia;
Italian forensic medicine professor Dr. Pier Baima Bollone of the
University of Turin; U.S. pathologist Dr. Frederick Zugibe, chief
medical examiner, Rockland County, New York; and U.S. coro-
ner Dr. Robert Bucklin of Los Angeles County, California. Dr.
Bucklin is said to be the real-life forensic scientist upon whom the
TV series "Quincy" is based.

Inevitably, because of the varying backgrounds of such men
and the already mentioned subtleties of the Shroud image, not all
agree on all details. Nonetheless, across their published findings
there is a broad consensus in identifying on the Shroud five distinct, major groups of injuries.

The first such group consists of variegated wounds to the head,
some distinct, others less so. Among the latter, but consistently
pointed out by Bucklin, Willis, and others, are a large swelling on
the upper right cheek, just below the eye, and similar damage to
the nose. Inferred from this damage is a heavy blow struck across
the face.

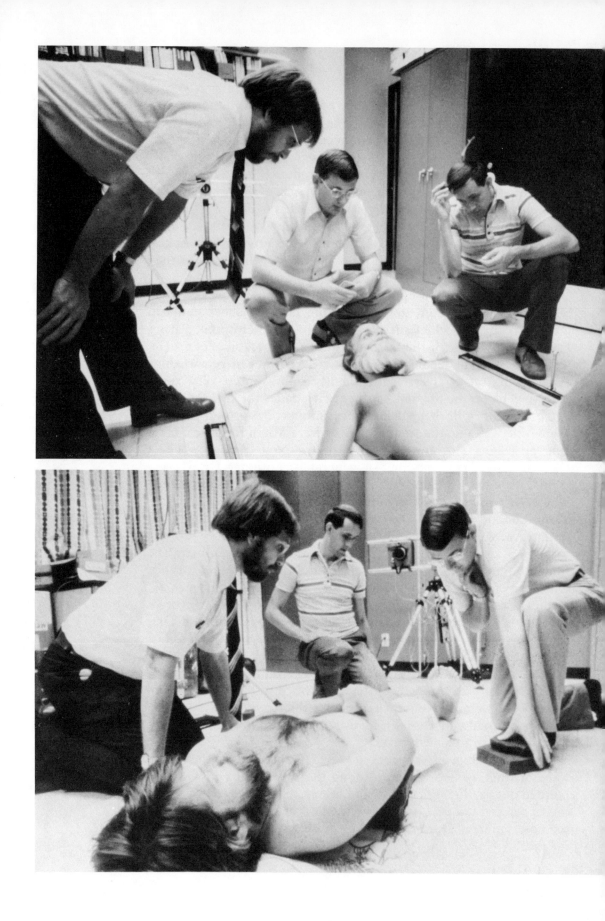

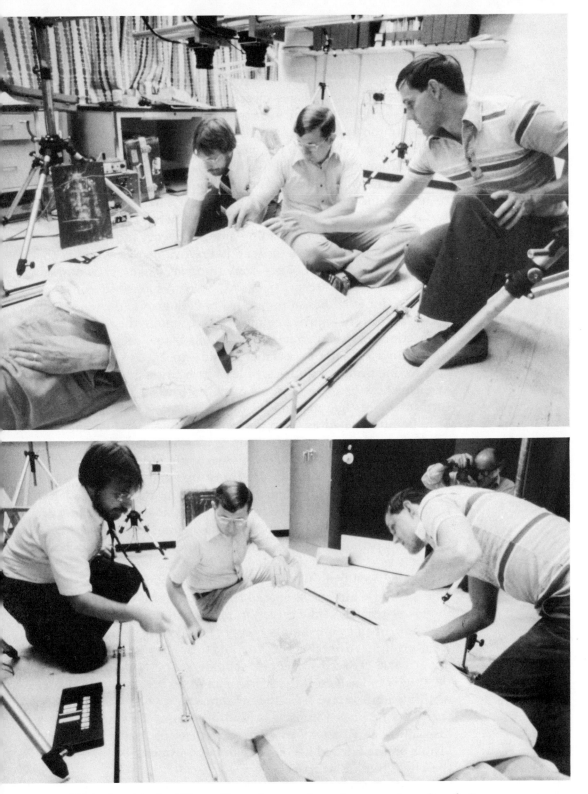

With the aid of a "Shroud" mock-up and a volunteer selected to fit it, Doctors Jackson and Jumper and colleagues reconstruct the original burial attitude of the man of the Shroud. Calculations of height and weight have been made possible by experiments of this kind.
(Vernon Miller)

Still in the same group, but far more obvious to the layman, are a series of blood spillages clearly visible around the front and back of the head. Four or five streams of blood seem to start from the top of the forehead moving downward toward the eyes. Other streams appear clotted in the hair. The face image has one particularly striking flow, shaped like a reversed figure 3, that starts just below the hairline, then meanders obliquely downward, seeming to meet some obstruction in its descent. The back of the head features some eight or more downward-flowing rivulets, each expanding and sometimes dividing along the way, and similarly being interrupted by some obstruction. Obvious to anyone is that some irregular spiked object—something very like a crown or cap of thorns—would seem to have been responsible for these wounds. But what has so impressed pathologists is the true-to-life appearance of the injuries. Some even see among the rivulets clear distinctions between arterial and venous blood, each behaving in the manner a modern specialist would expect.

A second group of injuries, of less variegation but much greater extensiveness, is to be seen all over the back of the body in the form of more than a hundred dumbbell-shaped marks that can only be interpreted as from a severe whipping. Individually the marks have been identified as contusions, or hematomas; that is, wellings of blood into the flesh tissues without necessarily breaking the skin. They occur in groups of two and three, and would appear to have been inflicted by a two- or three-thonged lash tipped with dumbbell-shaped metal pellets. If these are the work of a forger, it is, again, the thinking behind them that has so impressed pathologists. Goniometry is the science of calculating angles, that is, for instance, enabling the direction of fire of a rifle to be calculated from the path of a bullet through a victim's body. The Shroud whip marks spread from the tops of the shoulders to the lower reaches of the calves, in places extending to the front of the body, in an astonishingly convincing-looking distribution pattern. From horizontal across the loins they fan upward over the upper back, crisscross over the shoulders, and fan downward on the thighs and calves. If the work of a forger, he has taken the care to think out exactly how the whipmaster swung this way and that, how he placed himself behind his victim, how high he held his hand, yet all so subtly conveyed that the marks are hardly visible on the Shroud itself, and can only properly be followed on the photographic negative.

As noted by Professor Cameron, in the shoulder regions these injuries appear to have been succeeded by some major source of abrasion, evident from the appearance of rubbing high on the left

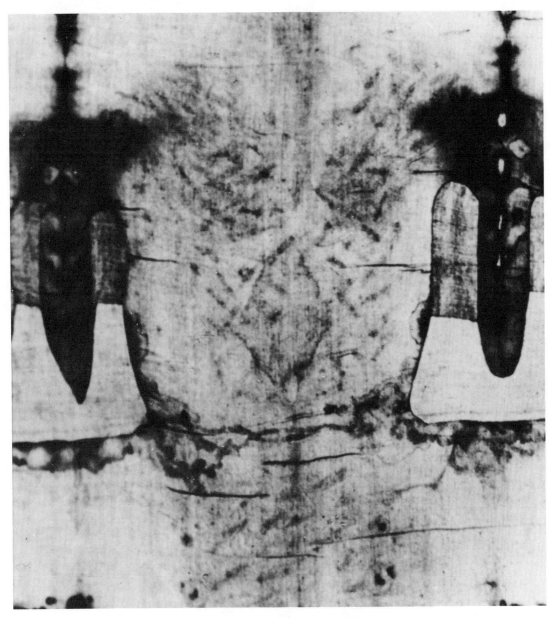

Back of body image, showing scourge marks. *(G. Enrie)*

shoulder blade and lower down on the right. Cameron interprets this as the carrying of some heavy weight on the back, inevitably recalling the cross or crossbeam carried by crucifixion victims, and points out, in likely association, apparent damage to the knees, particularly the left one. From experiments with volunteers, Cameron observes that a right-handed person with a heavy beam tied to his outstretched arms tends naturally to carry this high on his left shoulder, lower down on his right, and when he falls, this will be most heavily on his left knee. Again the Shroud makes sound medical sense.

For the first clear evidence that the Shroud shows a victim of crucifixion, we now turn to the next group of injuries, which take the form of what appear to be blood flows in the region of the hands and lower arms. On the man of the Shroud's left wrist can be seen two separately angled blood flows, one broad, the other thin and long; then, after a gap of a few centimeters, at least six blood rivulets appear to flow on toward the elbow joint. Although the right wrist is obscured by the left, the presence of similar bloodstains on this arm suggests a similarly originating injury. As before, it is the underlying logic that is so compelling. Each rivulet of blood ends its course pointing in a specific direction, from which it can be calculated that when the majority of the rivulets flowed, the man of the Shroud's arms must have been at an angle of 65 degrees from the vertical—i.e., clearly a crucifixion position. Only one rivulet is different, the longer and thinner of those at the wrist, which indicates not 65 but 55 degrees from the vertical. To pathologists, this single flow almost certainly indicates the attitude the arms assumed at death, at which time the head would have been slumped and one elbow flexed at a more acute angle.

If these features are remarkable enough, even more so is the location from which the two separately angled flows can be seen to emerge: the wrist. Throughout art history, the thousands of artists' representations of the crucifixion almost invariably show the nails through the palms, not the wrists. For the Shroud to feature such an unexpected location fascinated the French surgeon Pierre Barbet, and it was in order to try to understand this that he conducted some of his experiments on cadavers and amputated limbs during the 1930s. Replicating the suspension of a body via a nail through the palm, as imagined by artists, Barbet found that the flesh simply tore through. Such a location could not have supported a body on a cross. But when Barbet drove a nail through the point he judged to be indicated on the Shroud, the highly compacted metacarpal bones of the wrists, he found that any normal body weight was held firm and secure. Was a four-

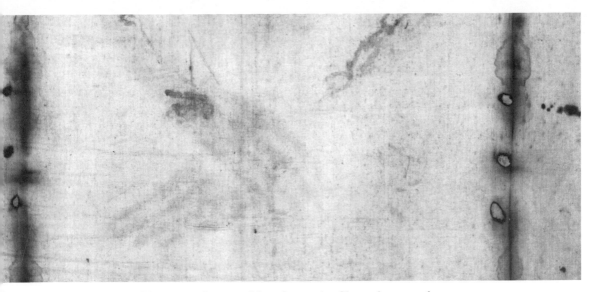

Above: Close-up of crossed hands on the Shroud, natural appearance, showing apparent entry point of nail in wrist. *(Vernon Miller)*

Below: Reconstruction of nail driven through bones of the wrist, with skeletal diagram at right. The nail passes through the meso-carpal space of Destot, which forms a natural anatomical tunnel. It has been calculated that the weight of the body would cause a traction of 95 kilograms on each hand. *(Dr. Robert Bruce-Chwatt)*

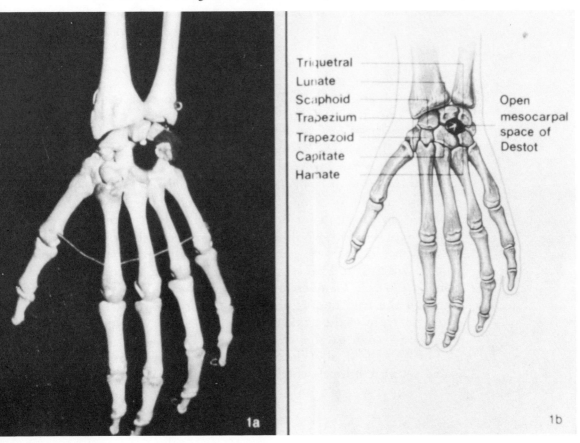

Triquetral
Lunate
Scaphoid
Trapezium
Trapezoid
Capitate
Hamate

Open mesocarpal space of Destot

1a

1b

teenth-century forger so clever that he defied artistic tradition to
get such an anatomical detail correct?

Some medical researchers have called into question certain
finer points of detail among Barbet's findings. Dr. Anthony Sava,
for instance, would locate the Shroud wrist nail through the wrist
end of the radius and ulna arm bones, while Dr. Frederick Zugibe
suggests that the nail was driven, at an angle, through the thenar
groove, at the base of the thumb, to emerge at the wrist. But the
exit point is agreed by all to be at the wrist, and few have seriously challenged this feature's essential convincingness.

Evidence of crucifixion is further to be found in the Shroud's
fourth group of injuries: blood flows that seem to denote nails
through the feet. Although little of any bloodstains at the front of
the feet are evident (as already remarked, at the front not enough
length would seem to have been allowed for the Shroud to stretch
the full distance to the toes), the back of the body image incorporates a very complete imprint of the sole of the right foot, seemingly soaked in blood, and with the uncanny appearance of the
sort of mark someone might leave if he stepped on a wet flagstone.
Anatomically, pathologists and other medical men have noted to
this image a very definite concavity corresponding to the foot's
plantar arch, also a dark, rectangular stain between what would
seem to have been the second and the third metatarsal bones,
seemingly the nail's entry point. Since only an almost indistinguishable smudge is visible for the left foot, it has been argued
that on the cross the right foot overlaid this, with a single nail
impaling the two.

From the ankle, a rill of blood appears to have broken away
directly onto the cloth, and it is the seemingly post-mortem nature of this that has caused most interest. While all previously
discussed bloodstains have theoretically flowed while the body
was upright on the cross, dried on the body, then somehow become transferred after death, this ankle rill must have been of a
different nature, presumably an accidental spillage as the body
was laid on the cloth for burial. There is even a counterimpres-
sion where the cloth would appear to have been slightly wrinkled
at the time. The fact of such an important spillage at the ankle is
itself of interest and has suggested to Philadelphia medical professor Dr. Joseph Gambescia that there were in fact two nails
through the feet, one as previously described, the other driven
from the front of the ankle through to the heel. Artistic tradition
offers no known parallel to a feature of this kind.

The fifth and final of the Shroud's visible injury groups is indicated by an elliptical wound 4.4 centimeters wide immediately

Close-up of foot wound on Shroud dorsal image, showing apparent entry point of nail, with, at the heel, a rill of blood that appears to have spilled directly onto the cloth as the man of the Shroud was laid in this. *(G. Enrie)*

Reconstruction of nail driven through bones of the feet, with skeletal diagram at right. With a nail lodged between the second and third metatarsal bones, the crucifixion victim would have been able to push down on this in order to ease the excruciating weight on his hands—but only at the price of fresh pain. *(Dr. Robert Bruce-Chwatt)*

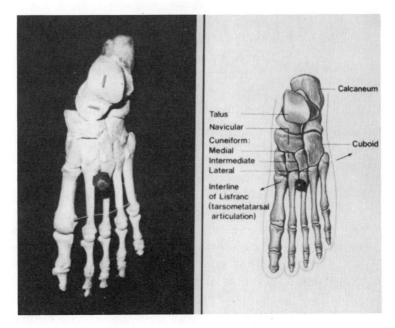

Calcaneum

Talus
Navicular
Cuneiform:
Medial
Intermediate
Lateral

Cuboid

Interline
of Lisfranc
(tarsometatarsal
articulation)

adjacent to one of the 1532 fire patches and, on the body of the
man of the Shroud, locatable in the right side. Even to the layman
this looks obvious as the entry point of some spear, from which
blood appears to have flowed for some 15 centimeters while the
body hung upright on the cross. But it is inevitably the pathologists for whom, again, the injury is most meaningful. There is
general agreement that the exact point of injury would have been
in the fifth intercostal space, immediately above the sixth rib, and
it is to be noted that the wound is angled perfectly for such a
between-the-ribs location. Some investigators even see slight in-
terruptions in the flow of the blood downward exactly corresponding to the spacings of the middle ribs. The most dramatic
aspect of this injury is that, as in the case of the foot wound, there
is a post-mortem spillage associated with it, in this instance in the
form of a copious and intricate splashing of blood visible right
across the small of the back on the dorsal image, extending out to
each side. Among the pathologists, there is general agreement
that this spillage would have occurred as the heavy body was
inevitably heaved onto the cloth at the time of burial.

If the Shroud is genuine, obviously such a dramatic chest injury must have been caused by a blow intended to cause death.
But, quite aside from this, doctors and pathologists have pointed
to other evidence that the man of the Shroud was indeed dead
when laid in the cloth. As Professor James Cameron of the London Hospital has observed, if the man of the Shroud had been still
breathing when laid in the cloth, the natural effect of his inhala-
tions would have been to suck the linen into his mouth and nos-
trils, as indeed occurred in one modern case which Cameron was
called upon to examine. This would inevitably have distorted the
Shroud facial image; yet it shows no sign of this. Cameron also
interprets the already noted stiffness of the arms in the burial
position as due to rigor mortis. He argues that the arms had become fixed in the attitude of their suspension on the cross, and
those who took the body down therefore had forcibly to break
this rigor at the shoulders in order to place the arms in the burial
position. Cameron also offers an interesting explanation for the
oddly skeletal appearance of the hands. He points out that a nail
through the wrist would be likely to hit not only the median
nerve but also the main artery, thereby partially draining the
hands of blood and creating an early post-mortem tissue-drying
effect he refers to as "de-gloving."

The single most overriding feature from the evidence of the
pathologists is, however, their unanimity that what they see of
wounds and physiological features on the Shroud makes perfect

Apparent chest wound on the Shroud, seen immediately to the left of one of the triangular patches sewn on by Poor Clare nuns. The wound's elliptical shape corresponds closely with that of a cross section of the Roman *lancea*, or lance. *(Vernon Miller)*

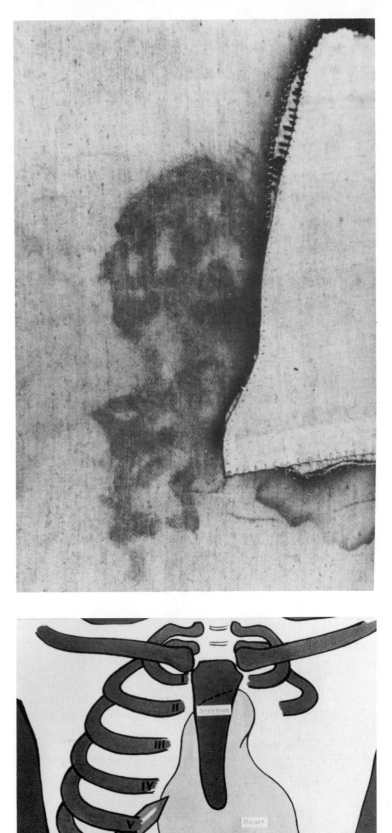

Reconstruction of entry point of lance, as transposed onto a human chest. The blade would have penetrated between the fifth and sixth ribs, and was clearly aimed at the heart. *(Holy Shroud Guild)*

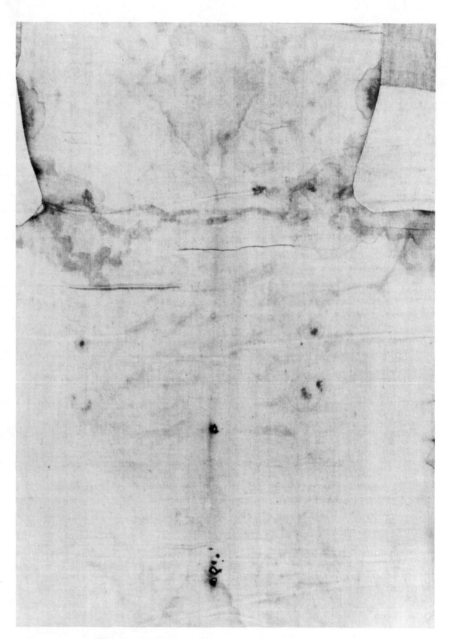

Apparent spillage of blood across the small of the back. This would appear to have come from the chest wound and to have dripped across the cloth as the body was being laid in the Shroud.
(Vernon Miller)

medical sense. The behavior of the blood flows, irrespective of whatever process might have transferred them to the cloth, is in precise accord with the observed injuries. There is one medical detractor, Dr. Michael Baden, deputy chief medical examiner for Suffolk County, New York, who argues that the Shroud is "too good to be true" and that "human beings don't make this kind of pattern," but he misses the point. No one fully conversant with the Shroud suggests other than that whatever created the perfection of the Shroud image was an unparalleled and as yet incompletely understood process. The essential issue is that the entire corpus of medieval and subsequent art can be scoured in vain for the work of any painter whose depiction of injuries even remotely approaches the realism of those visible on the Shroud. Although this does not prove the Shroud genuine, it acts as a powerful catalyst to further inquiry . . .

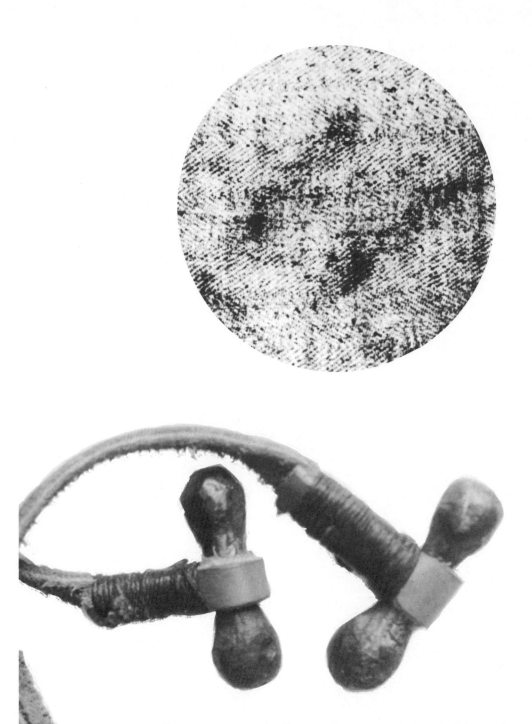

Reconstruction of a Roman *flagrum*, with detail of Shroud scourge marks. *(Vernon Miller)*

3

THE CASE FOR THE SHROUD'S ANTIQUITY

Only during the Renaissance did there begin even the glimmerings of a serious interest in archaeology. In the Middle Ages, artists usually had so little historical sense that they unhesitatingly clothed biblical characters in the costume of the artists' own time and set them amid Gothic architecture. A typical example is Flemish artist Dirk Bouts's *Arrest of Jesus*, painted about the middle of the fifteenth century. The soldiers arresting Jesus carry a most interesting selection of weapons: a spiky mace, a halberd, a pike, and a couple of variations on a spear—all of them thoroughly medieval. In Gerard David's *The Supper at Cana*, painted about fifty years later, we are offered a fascinating tableau of contemporary tableware, costume, wall hangings, and architecture; contemporary, that is, for David's Bruges, not for Jesus' Jerusalem.

It is therefore yet another fascinating feature of the Shroud that if its image is the work of an artist, he made no such normal artists' mistakes. As will be recalled from the discussion in the previous chapter concerning the whip injuries, each of these exhibits a specific, characteristic shape best described as like a dumbbell. So precise are these markings that where they fell true they even have identical dimensions, enabling a reconstruction of the device that theoretically originally caused them. They match the twin pellets of metal (or sometimes bone) typically affixed to the ends of the thongs of the Roman scourge, or *flagrum*, a particularly brutal, two- or three-thonged whip, of which examples have been excavated at Herculaneum. The Gospels, of course, specifically state a scourging was carried out on Jesus. If the Shroud image is the work of an artist, his archaeology was faultless.

A similar situation is to be found in the already noted location of the crucifixion nail in the wrist. Although, as already discussed, the wrist has seemed medically the logical point for sus-

31

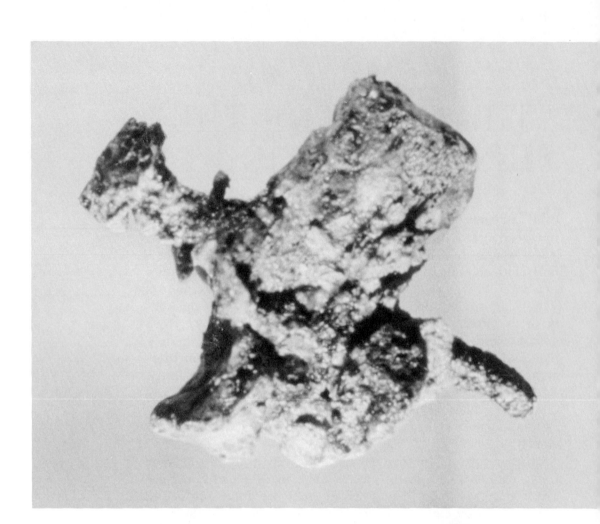

(Above) Nail through the anklebone of skeleton discovered by Israeli archaeologists at early Jewish cemetery excavated at Giv'at ha-Mivtar, northern Jerusalem. (Right) Reconstruction of how Giv'at ha-Mivtar victim was crucified, showing nails through the wrists. *(Dr. Patricia Smith, Hebrew University, Israel Exploration Journal)*

pending a body from a cross, until very recently there was no archaeological evidence to which anyone could look for independent corroboration. Although, for slaves and rebels, crucifixion was a common enough form of execution in antiquity, there was also a popular notion that the nails from such punishments were good for curing such varied disorders as epilepsy and bee stings. As a result, they would seem generally to have been removed from the body, leaving any subsequently excavated skeletons without obvious clues as to the cause of death.

Accordingly, of unusual interest in relation to the Shroud was the discovery, in 1968, of the first known actual skeletal remains of a crucifixion victim, found during excavation of a New Testament-period Jewish cemetery at Giv'at ha-Mivtar, just outside Jerusalem. As Israeli archaeologists opened one of this cemetery's ossuaries, or bone boxes, the first clue confronting them was a 17-to-18-centimeter-long iron nail transfixing the ankle bones of the skeleton of a young adult male. In a manner not dissimilar to the controversies surrounding the Shroud, the archaeologists and anatomists interpreting this skeleton have not agreed with each other concerning exactly how this victim was suspended on the cross.

According to one, the legs were forced into an awkward, sideways position. According to another, the crucifixion was upside down. According to yet another, the feet were nailed side by side to a loose platform, with another nail hammered through the ankles. Whatever the arrangement, some details of this crucifixion, such as the breaking of the legs, were different from those of the man of the Shroud. This is not surprising, as Roman crucifixions are known to have varied according to the whims of the local execution squad, St. Peter having been crucified upside down, and the legs broken of the robbers crucified with Jesus.

But what is important about the Giv'at ha-Mivtar victim is that, exactly as in the case of the man of the Shroud, he was suspended by the wrists. An unmistakable scratch on the radius bone shows that the nail must have been driven in at the wrist end of the radius and ulna bones, the very location favored in respect of the Shroud by New York's Dr. Anthony Sava. And if arguments for the platform mode of ankle nailing are accepted, then this would accord very well with the reconstruction of the foot-nailing of the man of the Shroud suggested by Philadelphia's Dr. Joseph Gambescia.

Still in the field of archaeology, another feature of some interest is the chest wound. As already mentioned, this has a very clear elliptical shape, and the dimensions are easily determinable: 4.4

centimeters long by approximately 1.1 centimeters wide. Such an injury corresponds very well to what might be expected from the Roman *lancea*, an elliptically bladed weapon intended for continuous use, such as by legionaries on a garrison posting. According to investigations made by U.S. researcher Paul Maloney of the *Biblical Archaeologist*, some surviving specimens of the Roman *lancea*, seen in cross section, match perfectly the dimensions of the Shroud wound. It is to be noted that it is quite specifically a *lancea*, the Greek form of which is λογχη, which the author of John's gospel describes as having been plunged into the side of Jesus as a check that he was dead.

Also at least worthy of mention is the burial attitude. Some writers, notably the Reverend Sox, have deemed the Shroud inauthentic because the arms appear placed modestly across the loins, rather than at the side of the body, but there appears no sound justification for this view. Attitudes varied in antiquity as they do today, and while, for instance, first-millennium B.C. Egyptian pharaohs had their arms placed alongside their hips, cadavers of the priestly caste were buried with hands across the loins. In Judea, a number of skeletons excavated in the Essene cemetery at Qumran (ca. 200 B.C. to A.D. 70) were laid out flat, facing upward, elbows bent slightly, and hands crossed across the pelvis, more or less exactly the attitude visible on the Shroud. In this context, it needs to be remarked that whatever the burial position adopted, this was usually only a temporary one. It was standard Jewish practice that when the deceased's flesh had fully rotted from his bones, they would be gathered up into an ossuary, just like the one in which the Giv'at ha-Mivtar crucifixion skeleton was found, the laying-out place then being ready for the next interment. Reliable information on interim burial positions is therefore of necessity slim.

Of all archaeological features, however, inevitably the prime and most crucial concern the linen of the Shroud and whether this could indeed be interpretable as from the Near East of the first century A.D. To try to answer this question, in 1973 two small linen samples (one 13 × 40 millimeters, the other 10 × 40 millimeters) were cut off from the Shroud and examined by Professor Gilbert Raes of the Ghent Institute of Textile Technology, Belgium. Raes quickly confirmed earlier opinions that the Shroud's fabric is linen, spun with a Z twist, and woven in a three-to-one (herringbone) twill. He noted the yarn to be very regular, indicative of good-quality workmanship, and the weave density an average of a little over 35 threads per centimeter (warp 38.6, weft 35.5), corresponding favorably with the 30-thread-per-

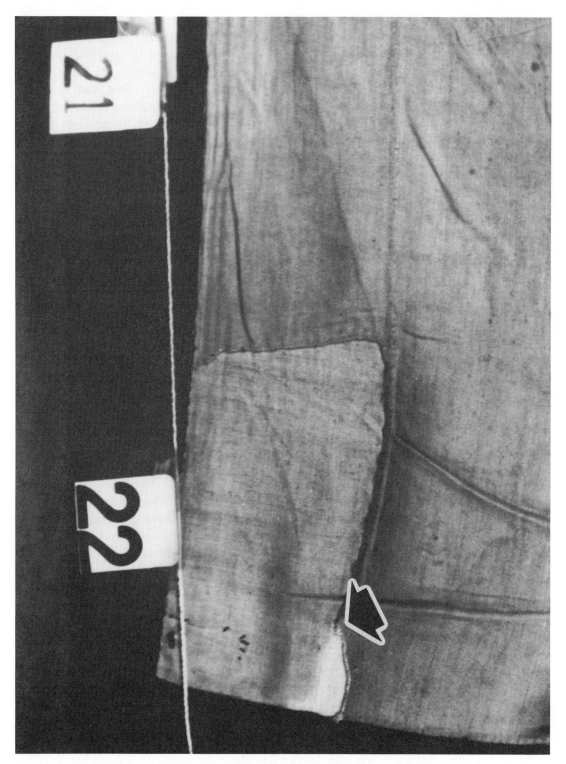

Corner of Shroud, showing point of removal (arrowed) of linen
sample for Professor Raes. *(Vernon Miller)*

centimeter average for the finest Egyptian mummy fabrics. Raes also found, mixed with the linen fibers, small traces of cotton.

One of the first unusual features of Raes's information is the Z twist. Despite large quantities of linen surviving from Egyptian tombs (365 square meters was measured from one Metropolitan Museum mummy alone), virtually invariably this has been spun S twist, i.e. with the spindle revolved counterclockwise. The Egyptian linen is also consistently in a plain weave (i.e., a simple one-over, one-under style), rather than the Shroud's more complex three-to-one twill.

These features do not, however, present any special difficulty. What is known of Egyptian linens, of which large quantities have been preserved, is by no means necessarily representative of Palestinian linens, of which examples are much more scarce. That a Z twist and twill weaving were practiced in times well before the first century A.D. is obvious from a late-Bronze Age cloak found at Gerumsberg, Germany. This has the additional feature of having been "woven without seam" (i.e., shaped by dropping warp ends as the weaving progressed), the identical characteristic noted by Gospel writer John in respect of the undergarment taken from Jesus at the time of the crucifixion. A third-century A.D. silk fragment from Palmyra, and another from a similarly dated child's coffin from Holborough, England, both feature the three-to-one twill weave and are thought to be of Syrian manufacture. It is also to be noted that although the Shroud linen is of Z twist, the thread used to sew the seam is in the more usual S twist. Z twist comes naturally to someone who is left-handed, and may simply indicate a left-handed spinner.

Perhaps the most curious feature of the Shroud samples studied by Raes is his observation that they included traces of cotton. These, of the Middle Eastern variety *Gossypium herbaceum,* suggest that, wherever the weaving of the Shroud was done, it was done on equipment also used for cotton. While this in turn suggests a Near or Middle Eastern manufacture, it has to be acknowledged that during the medieval period cotton was being produced in Italy, and cotton cloth was manufactured in France, Italy, and Flanders. Overall, Raes's evidence is ambivalent. It shows the Shroud could have been produced in first-century Palestine, but equally plausibly it could have been produced in fourteenth-century Europe or a fourteenth-century Muslim country, from which commercially expanding countries like France and Italy were importing heavily. Troyes, only twelve miles from Geoffrey de Charny's Lirey, was one of Europe's most important centers for precisely this form of trade.

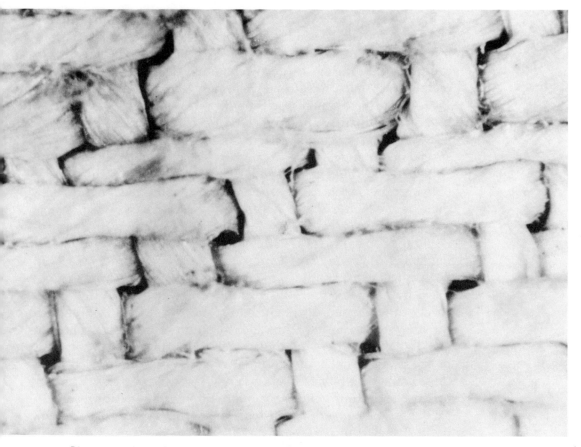

Close-up of the Shroud weave. Textile experts identify it as a three-to-one herringbone twill, more complex than the plain "one over, one under" weave most commonly found from the New Testament period. *(Vernon Miller)*

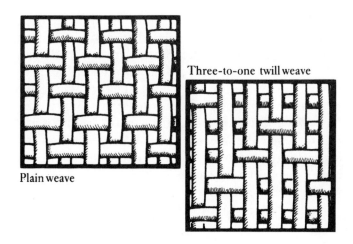

Three-to-one twill weave

Plain weave

But although, in the continued absence of a carbon-14 dating test, study of the Shroud's linen provides no sure way of determining whether it was produced in the first or the fourteenth century, one unusual modern technique does provide a way of establishing that the Shroud genuinely came from the East. In 1973, when the Shroud was brought out for a brief examination by a predominantly Italian group of scientists, Swiss criminologist Dr. Max Frei dabbed strips of sticky tape onto the cloth's surface in an endeavor to obtain samples of its dust, dust that he anticipated would include pollen grains. The special interest of pollen grains is that they have an exceptionally hard outer shell, the exine, which can last literally millions of years. What is very important is that this shell differs markedly in appearance according to the type of plant it has come from, enabling anyone analyzing pollen dust on, say, a murder suspect's clothing, to tell in what type of surroundings the garment has been worn. As recognized by Dr. Max Frei, this technique has a special value in respect of the Shroud. If the Shroud really was forged in France in the fourteenth century, then identification of exclusively French and Italian pollens would effectively confirm this. If, however, pollen grains from quite different regions were discovered, then these could be a powerful aid to understanding the cloth's earlier origins. Handling pollens for microscopic examination is a delicate and time-consuming business, but, from the samples he took in 1973 and a further batch in 1978, Frei managed to identify pollens from no fewer than fifty-eight varieties of plant, before his death in early 1983. The varieties of plant told their own striking story of the markedly differing geographical regions with which the Shroud had historically been associated, as is quite evident from the chart on pages 40 and 41.

Careful study of the table reveals, as might be expected, a substantial number of plant species that grow widely in France, Italy, and the general Mediterranean area. If pollens of these species alone had been found, there would be no justification for believing the Shroud to have been kept anywhere other than the places it is known to have been since the 1350s. In the case of one pollen, *Oryza sativa*, or rice, it is even possible, with some confidence, to name the specific town. Vercelli, where the Shroud is historically known to have been exhibited in 1494 and 1560, is Europe's principal rice-growing center. But as is also evident from the list, a similarly substantial number of pollens derive from steppe plants most commonly found in eastern Turkey. Two, *Atraphaxis spinosa* and *Prunus spartioides*, are virtually specific to this, while a further group, but most notably *Epimedium*

Swiss criminologist the late Dr. Max Frei, another European who
worked alongside the STURP team. His special interest was the
identification of pollens from the Shroud's dust, which he collected by
means of a sticky-tape dispenser. This unscientific-looking apparatus
aroused some criticism from STURP scientists Dr. Ray Rogers and
others. *(Barrie Schwortz)*

TABLE OF POLLENS FROM THE TURIN SHROUD as identified by Dr. Max Frei

Regions of provenance of the plants whose pollens have been found on the Shroud:

Alphabetic list of all the plants whose pollens have been found on the Shroud:

#	Plant	France, Italy	Mediterranean area	Istanbul environs	Anatolian Steppe	Jerusalem & environs	Iran-Turan	Arabia	Sahara	Regions of North Africa	Plant description
1	Acacia albida Del.					•				•	Plant of deserts. Most frequent around the Dead Sea
2	Alnus glutinosa Vill.	•									
3	Althaea officinalis L.	•	•			•					Halophyte
4	Amaranthus lividus L.	•									Love-lies-bleeding
5	Anabasis aphylla L.					•	•	•		•	Plant of deserts, halophyte. Frequent in South Palestine
6	Anemone coronaria L.		•			•					
7	Artemisia Herba-alba A.				•	•	•	•		•	Plant of semideserts. Most frequent in the east of Jerusalem
8	Atraphaxis spinosa L.				•		•				Plant of deserts: Iran, Turan, Anatolia
9	Bassia muricata Asch.					•					
10	Capparis spec.		•		•	•	•				Plant of semideserts. Frequent on rock debris and old walls (caper)
11	Carduus personata Jacq	•									Thistle
12	Carpinus betulus L.	•									
13	Cedrus libanotica Lk.	•	•	•		•					Cedar of Lebanon
14	Cistus credicus L.		•			•					Rock rose
15	Corylus avellana L.	•		•							Hazel
16	Cupressus sempervirens L.	•	•	•		•					Cypress
17	Echinops glaberrimus DC					•				•	Plant of deserts. Frequent in rocky debris
18	Epimedium pubigerum DC			•							Southeast Europe, Turkey
19	Fagonia mollis Del.					•		•	•		Plant of deserts. Frequent in the valley of the Jordan
20	Fagus silvatica L.	•									Beech
21	Glaucium grandiflorum B&H				•	•	•				Plant of steppes. Frequent in South Palestine
22	Gundelia Tournefortii L.				•	•	•				Plant of salt steppes
23	Haloxylon persicum Bg.					•	•				Plant of deserts, halophyte
24	Haplophyllum tuberculatum J.				•	•		•	•		Plant of deserts
25	Helianthemum versicarium B.				•	•	•			•	Plant of deserts and semideserts
26	Hyoscyamus aureus L.					•	•				Plant frequent on rocks, old walls, ruins. Frequent on the old walls of Jerusalem

Table of Shroud pollens identified by Dr. Max Frei. (*Based on an original chart by Prof. Dr. Werner Bulst, S.J.*)

	Regions of provenance of the plants whose pollens have been found on the Shroud: ➤ / Alphabetic list of all the plants whose pollens have been found on the Shroud: ▼	France, Italy	Mediterranean area	Istanbul environs	Anatolian Steppe	Jerusalem & environs	Iran-Turan	Arabia	Sahara	Regions of North Africa	Plant description
27	Hyoscyamus reticulatus L.				•	•	•				Plant of steppes. Frequent on ruins
28	Ixiolirion montanum Herb					•	•				Plant of steppes
29	Juniperus oxycedrus L.			•	•	•	•				Coniferous evergreen shrub (Juniper)
30	Laurus nobilis L.	•	•	•		•					Laurel
31	Linum mucronatum Bert.				•	•	•				Plant of limy steppes
32	Lythrum salicaria L.	•									
33	Oligomejus subulata Boiss.			•		•	•			•	Plant of sandy and limy deserts
34	Onosma syriacum Labill.					•	•				Plant of steppes and deserts. Frequent on the walls of old Jerusalem
35	Oryza sativa L.	•									Rice
36	Paliurus Spina-Christi Mill.		•			•	•				
37	Peganum Harmala L.				•	•	•			•	Plant of deserts
38	Phyllirea angustifolia L.		•			•					
39	Pinus halepensis L.		•			•					Pine
40	Pistacia lentiscus L.		•			•					Pistacia
41	Pistacia vera L.		•			•					Pistacia
42	Platanus orientalis L.	•	•	•	•	•	•				Oriental plane tree
43	Poterium spinosum L.		•	•		•					Plant of arid soils
44	Prosopis farcta Macbr.				•	•	•				Most frequent around the Dead Sea
45	Prunus spartioides Spach.				•						
46	Pteranthus dichotomus Forsk.				•	•	•			•	Plant of sand and limy deserts
47	Reaumuria hirtella J&Sp					•	•	•	•		Plant of salt steppes
48	Ricinus communis L.	•	•	•	•	•					Plant of steppes (castor-oil plant)
49	Ridolfia segetum moris		•			•					
50	Roemeria hybrida (L)DC			•	•	•	•				Plant of steppes
51	Scabiosa prolifera L.					•	•			•	Plant of arid soils
52	Scirpus triquetrus L.	•		•		•					Rush
53	Secale spec.	•									Rye
54	Silene conoida L.		•		•	•	•				Plant of steppes
55	Suaeda aegyptiaca Zoh.					•		•	•		Plant of salt steppes
56	Tamarix nilotica Bunge					•		•	•		Plant of salt steppes
57	Taxus baccata L.	•		•							Yew
58	Zygophyllum dumosum B.					•			•		Plant of deserts. Most frequent around the Dead Sea
	Total numbers	17	18	13	18	45	22	7	6	9	

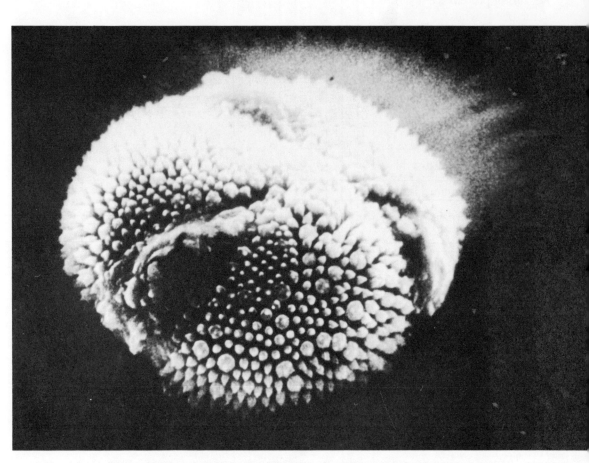

Pollen grain of the plant *Linum mucronatum*, one of a variety of non-European pollens found among Shroud dust by Dr. Max Frei. From this and other pollens, Dr. Frei concluded that the Shroud must have been in Anatolia and Israel at some time during its history. *(Dr. Max Frei)*

pubigerum, suggest some historical association with Istanbul, the former Constantinople. Further significance of these Turkish groups will become clear in Chapter 7.

Desert plants, most notably halophytes, specially adapted to grow in the exceptionally salty soil around the Dead Sea, also feature prominently in the list, along with no fewer than seven plants characteristic of Near Eastern rocky hills and other high places. It is obvious that the Shroud has been in a region typical of, if not identical with, the terrain in which the historical Jesus moved. But by far the greatest significance of the table is the preponderance of plants typical of, and in some cases effectively exclusive to, the environs of Jerusalem. The European representation is outweighed, the only reasonable inference being that it was somewhere in the Jerusalem region that the Shroud received its most prolonged exposure to the open air, pollens of course having less opportunity to migrate to the cloth as it hung in European churches or lay locked in their reliquaries.

As Frei argued, the Shroud therefore must have once been in the very region it has to have been if it wrapped the body of Jesus: the land we today call Israel. Perhaps inevitably, Frei's claims on this matter have not gone without criticism, even on the part of those otherwise convinced of the Shroud's authenticity. It has been pointed out, for instance, that dust can be carried great distances by the wind and by birds, Sahara dust having been blown to London, and Florida pollens to New York. Nonetheless, for such material to be blown from east to west would be contrary to all normal European wind patterns, and the proportions of Palestinian and Anatolian pollens identified by Frei are so high that it is unreasonable to attribute them to such chance circumstances.

Nor is Frei's scientific reputation easily assailed. Trained as a botanist, he was for twenty-five years head of the Zurich police's scientific laboratory, and after his retirement continued to be consulted by police forces from all over Europe. On the death of UN Secretary General Dag Hammarskjöld, he was appointed president of the fact-finding committee, and, as a Zwinglian Protestant, had not the slightest motivation for credulity toward Catholic relics, the one love of his life, outside his own family, being the study of botany. He died in March 1983 unwavering in his conviction of the validity of what he had found, and short of some as yet unthought-of anomaly, his researches deserve serious attention.

Establishment of the Shroud as of genuine Eastern provenance is still a long way, of course, from identifying it as of the time of Jesus, but nonetheless it is worth considering the various indications of its compatibility with what we might expect from Jesus and the Jewish world in which he moved. Although a forger would be expected to make the Shroud correspond with what can be read of his death in the Gospel accounts, the compatibility of the Shroud medical features with what is described in the Gospels is by any standards remarkable. This is best demonstrated in chart form, below.

WHAT THE SHROUD SHOWS	WHAT THE GOSPELS TELL
1. There appear to be a severe swelling below the right eye, and other facial injuries.	1. Jesus was struck a blow to the face (Mt. 27:30; Mk. 15:19; Lk. 22:63; Jn. 19:3).
2. Apparent bloodstains on the forehead and all around the back of the head show something spiked was forced onto the head.	2. Jesus was crowned with thorns (Mt. 27:29; Mk. 15:17; Jn. 19:2).
3. The body is literally covered with the wounds of a severe scourging.	3. Jesus was scourged (Mt. 27:26; Mk. 15:15; Jn. 19:1).
4. Scourge marks on the shoulders look blurred, as if something heavy has rubbed on them.	4. Jesus had to carry a heavy cross (Jn. 19:17).
5. The knees look as if they were injured by repeated falls.	5. Jesus' cross had to be carried for him (Mt. 27:32; Mk.15:21; Lk. 23:26), suggesting that he fell repeatedly because he was weak from his previous injuries.
6. There are apparent blood flows as from nail wounds in the wrists and feet.	6. Jesus was crucified by nailing in his hands and feet (Jn. 20:25 suggests this).
7. There is no sign that the legs were broken.	7. Jesus' legs were not broken (Jn. 19:33).
8. There is an elliptical wound, as from a lance, in the right side of the chest.	8. A lance was thrust into Jesus' side to check that he was dead (Jn. 19:34).

One of the most unexpected scholars to find the Shroud convincing was the late Dr. John Robinson, Dean of Trinity College, Cambridge, whose controversial *Honest to God* caused a rattling in many a British vicarage teacup during the 1960s. As pointed out by Dr. Robinson, the Shroud is very compatible with the clean linen *sindon* which the synoptic writers describe having been purchased for Jesus' burial by Joseph of Arimathea. And while the Gospel of John complicates matters by using different Greek words, of imprecise meaning, to refer to the cloths found in the tomb of Jesus after the disappearance of the body, this is not an overwhelming difficulty. John refers, for instance, to a *soudarion* that had been over Jesus' head "not with the linen cloths, but rolled up in a place by itself." Although this may have been a mere chin band, it implies a more substantial-size piece of linen, and an alternative interpretation is that it could have been the Shroud we know today. The root meaning of *soudarion* is sweat cloth, and the Shroud may have been intended as a temporary wrapping to soak up the sweat and blood from the body prior to a more definitive burial, which would have taken place after the Passover Sabbath.

Perhaps the most difficult feature, from the point of view of identifying the Shroud with Jesus and with a first-century Jewish burial, is that, quite clearly, the blood was not washed away from the body, and among almost all cultures, but most especially that of the Jews, washing was a standard preliminary to any burial. The usual counter to this argument has been that in Jesus' case, because his death was immediately prior to the Passover Sabbath (a specially holy day, when all work had to cease), Joseph of Arimathea had time only to arrange a preliminary burial. The washing of the body would therefore have been intended to take place on the day after the Sabbath (Easter Sunday) and was probably the mission of the women whom the Gospel writers describe hurrying to Jesus' tomb very early on that Sunday morning.

But what may be a far more satisfactory explanation has recently been suggested by Dr. Gilbert Lavoie of Massachusetts, who has noted that the *Code of Jewish Law* has some very special provisions for those who were victims of a bloody and violent death:

One who fell and died instantly, if his body was bruised and blood flowed from the wound, and there is apprehension that the blood of the soul was absorbed in his clothes, he should not be cleansed, but they should inter him in his garments and boots, but above his garments they should wrap a sheet which

is called *sovev*. It is customary to dig the earth at the spot where
he fell, if blood be there or nearby, and all that earth upon
which there is blood should be buried with him.

Although the text cited by Dr. Lavoie is sixteenth-century, present-day Jewish scholars such as Victor Tunkel of the London
University Faculty of Laws have expressed their support for Dr.
Lavoie's contention that the thinking behind the nonwashing of a
bloodstained body goes back to the very time of Jesus. It is linked
with the Pharisaic belief in physical resurrection of the body (de-
nied by the Sadducees), by which it was important that the whole
body, including spilled blood, be kept together for a complete
rising from the grave at the end of the world. On this reasoning it
would have been quite deliberate for Jesus' body not to be
washed, because of the violent and bloody nature of his death. As
a Jew, Victor Tunkel, for one, finds the absence of washing of the
man of the Shroud's body particularly compelling evidence for
the cloth's authentic Jewishness.

What, then, should be concluded concerning the antiquity of
the Shroud? No more than that, on the face of it, the Shroud
appears compatible with what might be expected for the time of
Jesus, assuming that there is some nonartistic explanation for the
image. The only properly definitive method of establishing the
Shroud to be of first-century date would be the carbon-dating
test, routinely used by archaeologists to date ancient organic materials such as wood, bone, and linen, but, so far, for reasons that
will be discussed in the last chapter, this has not yet been carried
out. Much, much more highly significant scientific work has,
however, been done, notably by an American team granted special access to the Shroud after the expositions of 1978, and it is to
this that we will now turn . . .

10. Shroud of Turin Research Project scientists smooth out wrinkles immediately prior to commencing their Shroud test program in Turin. The cloth is on the special aluminum frame designed to support it in both vertical and horizontal positions. *(Vernon Miller)*

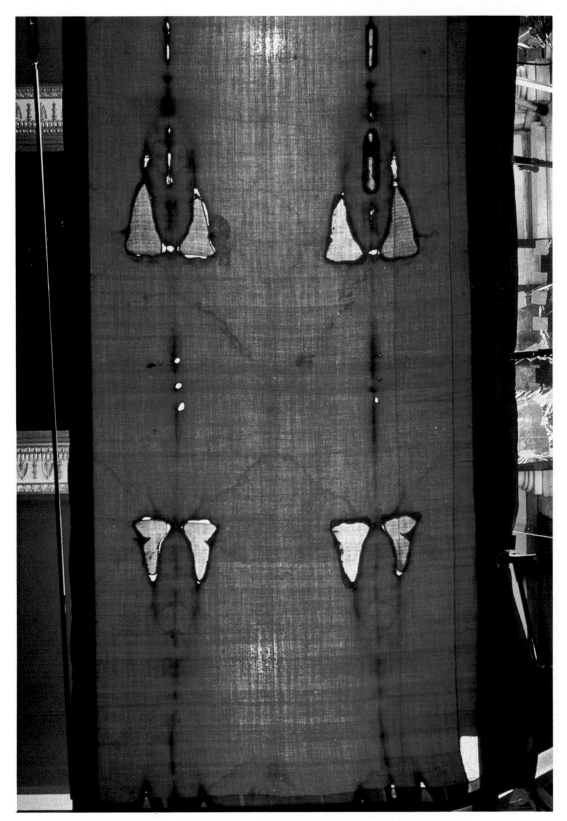

11. **Frontal and dorsal views of the Shroud, seen via transmitted light.**

Illuminated from behind, the damage from the 1532 fire shows up more
transparently than the unaffected areas (due to the greater opacity of the
Poor Clare nuns' patches), with holes in the cloth appearing white. Of special

12. Dorsal view of the Shroud, seen via transmitted light.

interest is the manner in which the alleged bloodstains show up dark, indicating the presence of some form of solid matter, while the body image virtually disappears. *(Barrie M. Schwortz)*

13. STURP optical physicist Sam Pellicori examines the Shroud with a binocular microscope specially adapted for vertical viewing. *(Vernon Miller)*

14. Photomicrograph of burn area on Shroud, showing how charring has run through the threads. *(Vernon Miller)*

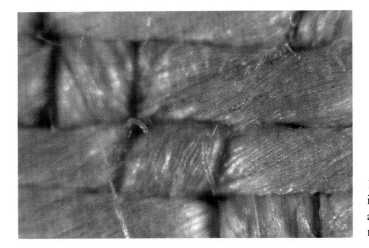

15. Photomicrograph of body image area on Shroud showing apparent absence of particulate matter. *(Vernon Miller)*

16. Photomicrograph of blood image area on Shroud showing what is indisputably some form of particulate matter. *(Vernon Miller)*

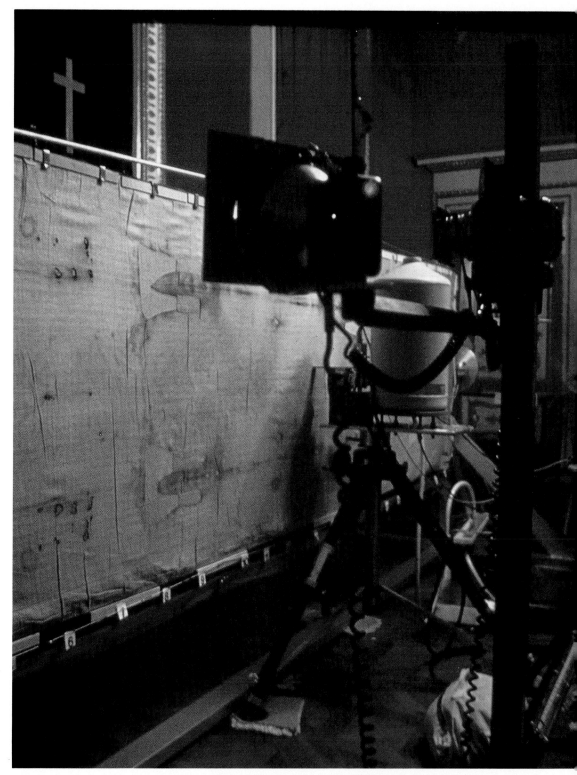

17. The Shroud illuminated during the ultraviolet fluorescence photography carried out by members of the STURP team in 1978. *(Barrie Schwortz)*

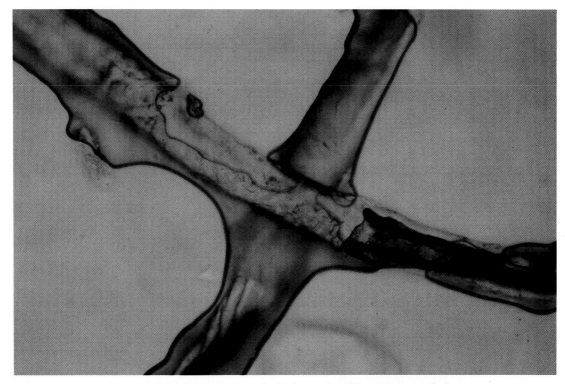

18. Close-up of a body-image fibril from the Shroud magnified 400 times. Notice its distinctive "corroded" appearance. *(Dr. Alan Adler)*

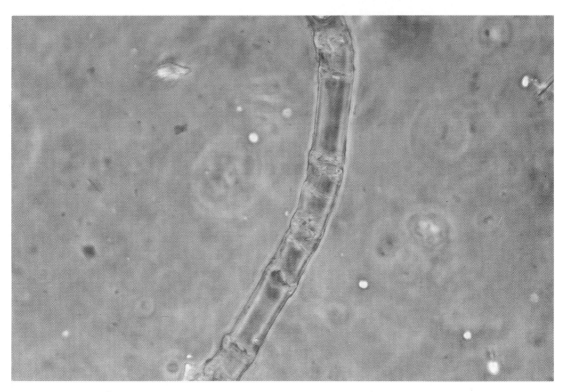

19. Close-up of a nonbody-image fibril from the Shroud magnified 400 times. Here notice its intact appearance when compared to the body-image fibril. *(Dr. Alan Adler)*

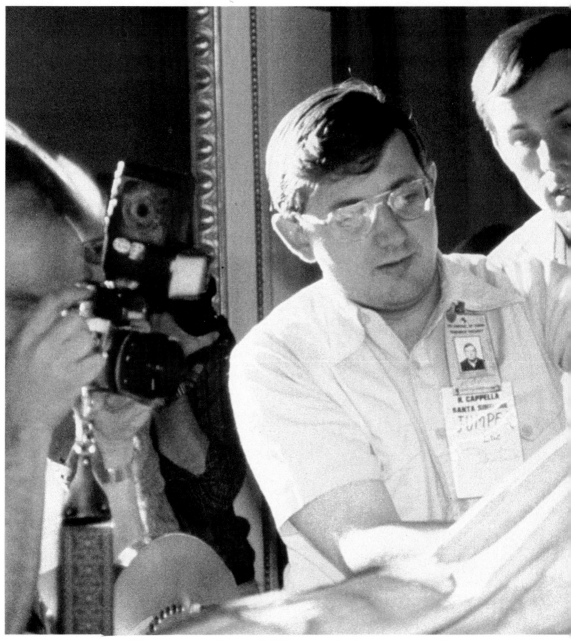

20. Photographer Vernon Miller records the moment as Doctors Jackson and Jumper examine the underside of the Shroud for the first time. *(Ernest Brooks)*

4

THE 1978 SHROUD TESTING

February 19, 1976, was a day physicist Dr. John Jackson will never forget. Today a research professor at Kaman Sciences in Colorado, in 1976 he was a U.S. Air Force captain serving as an instructor at Albuquerque, New Mexico. Ever since he was a teenager, he had been interested in the Shroud as a hobby, and, with fellow instructor Dr. Eric Jumper, had produced a full-size, carefully marked replica of the cloth designed for experiments to try to gain a better understanding of how the image might have been formed. On the nineteenth, he happened to call on the nearby Sandia Scientific Laboratories at Albuquerque, entering into a discussion of his Shroud experiments with an industrial radiographer, Bill Mottern, who happened at that time to be experimenting with a new piece of equipment, an Interpretation System's VP–8 Image Analyzer, recently developed as a spin-off from the NASA space research.

The special feature of Mottern's Analyzer was that it translated light and shade, as on a black-and-white photograph, into relief, viewable "in the round" on a television monitor. In the space-program work, two photographs taken from differing angles on the surface of the Moon could be fed into the machine and seen in their original relief on the television screen, an effect normally impossible in the case of a single photograph, such as a human portrait, which would be expected to contain insufficient relief information.

At the time of Jackson's visit, Mottern had not even heard of the Shroud, but as the two men discussed it, he suggested that, although he did not expect anything meaningful, it might at least be interesting to see what his machine made of it. It was therefore with some astonishment that, after the Shroud negative had been placed in the Analyzer, the two scientists found themselves looking at a convincing, properly three-dimensional image which could be consistently rotated without distortion, the only anomalies being creases and the 1532 fire marks (color plates 6 and 7). It was as if the Shroud, in addition to or alongside its negative char-

VP8 Image Analyzer view of Shroud frontal and dorsal images, showing their clear three-dimensional character. See also color photographs 6 and 7. *(Dr. John Jackson)*

acteristics, was somehow encoded with relief information of the body it once wrapped, which the Analyzer could reconvert back into its original form. As subsequent experiments revealed, no paintings produced the same effect under the Analyzer. For John Jackson it was visual confirmation that there was something quite extraordinary about whatever image-forming process was responsible for the Shroud image. In subsequent years, with colleagues he would go to the length of producing full-size statues of what the VP8 Image Analyzer "sees," one of which has recently been presented to the cardinal archbishop of Turin, and another to Pope John Paul II.

But even back in 1976 the discovery was, for Jackson, a revelation not dissimilar to the way he thought Pia must have felt when he first set eyes on the hidden Shroud negative nearly eighty years before. And while he and Eric Jumper were still in the first flush of excitement about this, the world's press suddenly announced startling new information from Turin concerning the Shroud. The small group of predominantly Italian scientists who, with Dr. Max Frei, had made a relatively cursory examination of the Shroud in 1973 had at last published their findings, a 120-page document entitled *La S. Sindone: Ricerche e studi della Commissione di Esperti* (The Holy Shroud: Research and Studies of the Commission of Experts). The Italians acknowledged some disappointments in their work. Using the standard peroxidase tests, for instance, they had not been able to determine the presence of blood on the Shroud. But neither had they been able to detect the presence of any obvious pigments, such as an artist would use. And, announced independently of the report, there were Dr. Max Frei's pollen findings.

It seemed obvious that after years of obscurity—it was already forty-five years since the Shroud had last been exhibited—a wave of new interest in the Shroud was about to begin, exemplified by an enthusiastic young British film producer, David Rolfe, who even at that time was making plans for what was to become the award-winning television documentary on the Shroud, *The Silent Witness*. As Jackson and Jumper kindled enthusiasm for their work among a variety of other scientists throughout the United States, they also strengthened an acquaintance with Father Peter Rinaldi, Italian-born pastor of Corpus Christi Church, Port Chester, New York, who had seen the Shroud for himself in 1933 and written articles and books on the subject ever since. In the hopes of promoting an exposition and international scientific examination of the Shroud, Rinaldi for many years had patiently nurtured diplomatic links both with the Shroud's formal owner, ex-king Umberto of Savoy, and with its executive custodian, Cardinal Michele Pellegrino, archbishop of Turin. A cardinal of the old school, Pellegrino had largely turned a deaf ear, even the cursory scientific examination of 1973 having been conducted in quite unnecessary secrecy. But, early in 1977, Rinaldi learned that Pellegrino, now approaching seventy-five, was about to retire later in the year, to be replaced by the altogether more progressive Archbishop Anastasio Ballestrero, from Bari.

The very next year, 1978, was the four-hundredth anniversary of the Shroud's arrival in Turin, and accordingly there could be no better time for one of the traditional, once-a-generation public expositions, accompanied on this occasion by a really definitive scientific testing. Losing no time to make his recommendations known to the Turin ecclesiastical authorities, Rinaldi simultaneously encouraged Jackson, Jumper, and their recently acquired colleagues to set down on paper exactly the type of testing work they would like to do on the Shroud, avoiding anything that might subject the cloth to unnecessary risk or damage. After a preliminary meeting in Turin, Rinaldi personally submitted the American proposals to the new cardinal, a man of warmth and decisiveness, and almost to their disbelief, Jackson and Jumper learned that they had been accepted. But the news also carried its own special responsibility: within a critically short time and with no ready-made financial backing, a relatively youthful group of scientists, scattered in various locations across the States and all with their own demanding daytime occupations, had to get together a project of pipe-dream complexity and take it nearly halfway across the world.

Given such difficulties, the group acted with admirable professionalism. Lacking any official sponsorship, they formed themselves into the Shroud of Turin Research Project (STURP), a tax-deductible corporation managed by an entrepreneurial Connecticut nuclear physicist, Tom D'Muhala. In every field in which they sought special expertise, they found individuals ready to join them, at their own expense, for the sheer interest value of the project. The VP8 Image Analyzer discovery had so intrigued Bill Mottern that he unhesitatingly volunteered his services for performing X-radiography of the Shroud, a task undertaken in association with Los Alamos National Scientific Laboratory stalwarts Ron London and Roger Morris. The image-enhancement and image-analysis skills generated by the NASA space program had to be useful for better understanding of the Shroud, and John Jackson delightedly received the support of Mars Lander-program veteran Don Lynn of Pasadena's Jet Propulsion Laboratory, along with associate Don Devan of Information Science Inc. from Santa Barbara, California. Spectroscopy, the science of analyzing objects of unknown chemical composition from the wavelengths of the radiation given off, was another field in which Jackson and Jumper hoped to gain valuable data, Connecticut's Oriel Corporation dutifully furnishing as specialists the husband-and-wife team Roger and Marion Gilbert. In the field of chemistry, the team found a veteran specialist, with some accompanying experience of archaeology, in Dr. Ray Rogers, working in thermal chemistry at the Los Alamos National Scientific Laboratory. Although the Shroud had been photographed both in color and in black and white by the Italians, Jackson and Jumper recognized the need for far more definitive and readily available photographic coverage, receiving enthusiastic support from Brooks Institute of Photography president Ernest H. Brooks, along with senior staff member Vernon Miller and Institute-trained photographers Barrie Schwortz and Mark Evans, all from Santa Barbara, California. Close by, the Santa Barbara Research Center furnished optical physicist Sam Pellicori, who was to apply himself particularly to what might be learned from ultraviolet fluorescence and low-power macroscopic photography of details of the Shroud images. For coping with all the electrical power problems that were inevitable with so many items of sophisticated American scientific equipment being brought to Italy, Jackson and Jumper looked to their well-trusted air-force colleagues Dee German and Rudy Dichtl of the Air Force Weapons Laboratory.

Besides personnel to be recruited, there was equipment to be obtained, always with the necessity for minimal expense. So that the Shroud could be securely held both horizontally and vertically during the various planned test programs, a metal frame was custom-built to the Shroud's full dimensions, complete with special magnetic holding strips and a detachable panel system for X-ray plates to be applied from behind. An individually designed adhesive-tape applicator was constructed for the removal of tiny samples of the Shroud's body and blood images; a special pure-hydrocarbon adhesive tape was formulated by the 3M company for use with this. Kodak provided a seemingly inexhaustible supply of film. The Brooks Institute of Photography provided expert photographic personnel, principal among these president Ernest Brooks and chief photographer Vernon Miller. Numerous routine items of scientific equipment for such purposes as photomicrography, X-radiography, and X-ray fluorescence analysis, were begged and borrowed from government and other institutions.

So in October 1978, after months of effort, the Shroud of Turin Research Project, comprising some twenty-four scientific and

STURP team members sort out some of their testing equipment in one of the elaborately decorated rooms made available to them within Turin's Royal Palace. *(Barrie Schwortz)*

technical personnel, many accompanying wives and children, and some eighty crates of equipment, found themselves in Turin, accommodation address the Hotel Sitea, working address a visiting prince's suite within the former Royal Palace. Grand though the team's working quarters sounded (and indeed looked), they scarcely offered the practicality the Americans would have wished. Lighting was by chandelier, bits of paint dropped from the ornately frescoed ceilings, mysterious breezes wafted through adjoining corridors, the floors were wood-block and uneven, and not least, power supplies were hopelessly inadequate.

Predictably, Italian officialdom, awed at the scale of the American equipment, announced that they were impounding it for sixty days, requiring frenetic diplomatic moves to get it released. Photographer Vernon Miller's independently dispatched consignment of dry-cell power packs failed to arrive, eventually being located in Milan. In such circumstances, of necessity the team members rapidly learned improvisation. In need of a darkroom for on-the-spot processing, Mottern and his radiographers took over and adapted the princely lavatory for the development of X-ray plates. Miller temporarily borrowed a *National Geographic* photographer's power pack. Electricity-supply specialists Dichtl and German, faced with a host of problems, teamed up with Torinese electrical technician Franco Faia. Amid all the problems, a most welcome "Mr. Fix-it" proved to be Turin University physicist Professor Luigi Gonella, fluent in English, principal scientific adviser to the Cardinal, and not least, as a specialist in both physics and engineering, sympathetic to the Americans' technical problems. After a frantic forty-eight hours, all essential equipment was powered and ready.

At last, late in the evening of Sunday, October 8, the final day of the six-week period of expositions to the public, a specially deputed group of young Italians removed the Shroud from its showcase and carried it, still tacked to its supporting piece of plywood, into the ornate but now cluttered and cable-strewn suite where the Americans sat waiting. With them for any stitching or unstitching that might be necessary were a small group of Sisters of Saint Joseph, together with some inquisitive Turin clergy and a handful of European specialists including Dr. Max Frei. Only since their arrival in Turin had the Americans learned that they would be allowed five days to carry out their tests but that the time would have to be shared with the Europeans.

Nerves were taut, and during the opening hours U.S.-European relations came under strain. Having spent much time and expense on the devising of their own ultrasophisticated sticky-tape dispenser, Jackson and his colleagues eyed with scarcely disguised contempt Dr. Max Frei's somewhat haphazard use of a homely roll of Scotch tape. Similar misgivings accompanied their viewing of Turin professor Aurelio Ghio's attempts at close-up photography with a flashgun held merely inches above the Shroud's surface. Only with the turn of Turin microanalyst Giovanni Riggi did American respect for European competence begin to improve. Dressed in a spotless white laboratory coat, Riggi had set himself the task of collecting in a special mini vacuum cleaner whatever loose dust might lie on the Shroud's surface. As his work would show, to study such dust under the microscope is to glimpse, albeit imperfectly, a cross section of the Shroud's history. There is power-station fly ash, testimony to the less than perfect methods used to conserve the Shroud within a twentieth-century industrial city. There are specks of various metals—iron, bronze, silver and even gold—attributable to the variety of containers and ecclesiastical ornaments with which the Shroud has been associated over the centuries. Conspicuous blackening of some of the silver fragments identify these with little doubt as from the melted casket in which the Shroud was kept at the time of the 1532 fire. Minute fabric particles attest to the variety of ecclesiastical vestments and more humble apparel that have brushed against the Shroud during the many public expositions. The high incidence of red and blue silk among these is readily traceable to the Shroud's traditional red cover and blue fabric surround. As in almost any cloth, Riggi found the remains of tiny *acari*, or mites, indicating that the Shroud is not immune from insect infestation.

When the Americans, in carefully ordered groups, took their turns at the cloth, some surprises became apparent. Having anticipated that the linen would be near to falling apart (even though the 1973 Commission had reported otherwise), the first cautious handling revealed the Shroud to be strong and resilient. Routine measurement with a micrometer established it to be approximately a third of a millimeter thick, slightly thicker than the holland cloth used to give it a backing after the 1532 fire.

Although much of the work involved the collection of data that it would take years to sift and analyze back in their laboratories, for some at least there was the opportunity of more immediate findings. In order not to lose their work going through airport X-ray machines, it was necessary for radiographer Bill Mottern and his colleagues to develop their sectional plates of the Shroud on the spot. Immediately, there showed up the thitherto unknown feature that the holland cloth is not one single length of

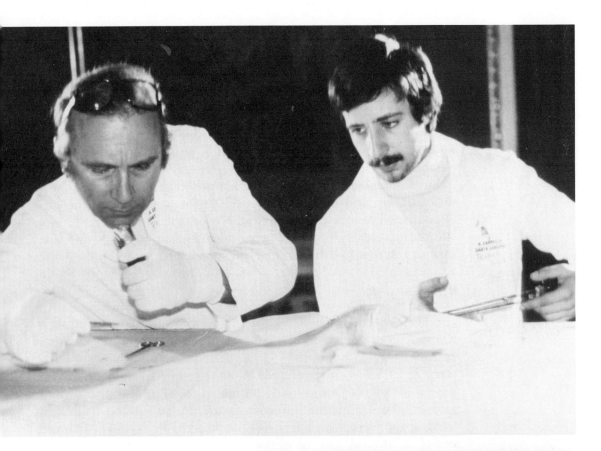

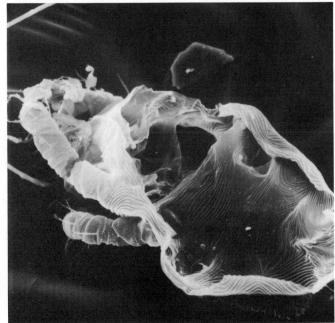

Above: Italian microanalyst Giovanni Riggi (left), who worked alongside members of the STURP team in 1978, with (right) the remains of one of several microscopic insects *(acari)* found by Riggi in the Shroud's dust. *(Vernon Miller, Giovanni Riggi)*

fabric, but what were originally three separate pieces sewn together in order to match the Shroud's dimensions.

Also revealed for the first time since the 1532 fire were the
substantial holes burnt into the linen, which the Poor Clare nuns'
patches had disguised. In one instance there were two holes below a single patch, and clearly disclosed in some places were signs
of where nuns had folded under the edges of patches in order to
form smooth edges prior to stitching, and other places where
patches were made a little too small to cover the holes completely.

But the real surprise was what happened to the Shroud's mysterious body and blood images. While features such as the lozenge-shaped stains from the water used to douse the 1532 fire
showed up clearly under X ray, nothing of either body or blood
images was at all visible, in marked contrast to the often dramatic
way in which artists' pigments show up in the radiography of old
masters.

A further element in the puzzle showed up in the course of
another experiment which provided on-the-spot data. While the
Shroud hung perpendicular on its test frame, the team set up a
battery of lights behind the cloth, their cameras in front, for the
purpose of what they referred to as transmitted-light photography (color plates 11 and 12). Illuminated from behind, the Shroud
glowed like a huge color transparency, but what the team was
looking for were which features blocked the light and which did
not. The Shroud was, of course, still affixed to its backing cloth,
and as in the X rays, the damage from the 1532 fire showed up
clearly, both patches and backing cloth exhibiting far more transparency than the Shroud itself. But especially notable was that, as
in the X rays, the body image effectively disappeared, but the
blood images, such as the chest wound, the wrist wound, the
trickles down the arms, etc., all showed up dark against the light.
The only plausible inference was that some quite strongly opaque
substance was acting as a block to the light in the blood areas, and
that this was responsible for what the eye saw as a bloodstain.
Clearly it would be a crucial part of the team's work to establish
precisely what this was.

For such a purpose, Jackson and his team had certainly not
come unprepared. Yet another routine but highly sophisticated
piece of equipment they had brought with them was a Wild M400
Photomakroscope, specially adapted to view and photograph the
tiniest details on the Shroud's surface as the cloth hung in the
perpendicular mode. The team member principally responsible
for this aspect was optical physicist Sam Pellicori from the Santa
Barbara Research Center (color plate 13). Having already ob-

Radiographer Bill Mottern (left) examines one of his team's X-ray photographs of the Shroud. *(Vernon Miller)*

Torque applicator being used to obtain image samples. *(Vernon Miller)*

served with ordinary eyesight how, the closer the Shroud's body image is viewed, the more it seems to melt into the cloth, Pellicori tried training the Photomakroscope on some of the more intense areas of body image, such as the tip of the nose. He found himself little the wiser. Focused on mere fibrils of threads, he could see not the slightest sign of any overlying pigment, all that the eye registered as body image seeming to derive from a slightly increased yellowing in comparison to those fibrils which could be interpreted as plain cloth. Whatever could have been responsible for such a yellowing seemed a complete mystery.

But it was a different story when Pellicori turned to what appear on the Shroud as bloodstains. At 32 × magnification under the Photomakroscope, he found himself looking at what was indisputably some form of particulate matter, tiny orange-red incrustations that seem to be caught in fibrils and crevices of the Shroud's threads. Could they be blood? They seemed unusually red for the brown color normally assumed by blood after any length of time, but the only satisfactory way of positively identifying blood was by chemical analysis in a laboratory. Using the special applicator, the American team was allowed to take sticky-tape samples from blood areas and, for comparison purposes, from body-image areas, water-stain areas, scorch areas, and nonimage areas. It was Dr. Ray Rogers, the thermal chemist from Los Alamos, who took charge of this particular task, and as he worked, he noticed that the fibers from the body image seemed to be removed more easily than those from nonimage areas. It was as if whatever process created the body image had in some way slightly weakened the Shroud fibers at these points. Yet another matter for the chemical analysts! As soon as they had been removed, the sample-bearing tapes were affixed sticky-side downward to glass microscope slides, careful notes being made of the points from which they had been removed, then packed into containers to await transport to the U.S.A.

Before this and other appointed tasks could be considered complete, there was one further question that needed answering. Since 1534, when the Poor Clare nuns sewed on the backing cloth, no one had been able to examine the Shroud's underside to determine whether the body and blood images penetrated the cloth or lay on the surface only. Graciously the Italian clergy gave permission for the Sisters of Saint Joseph to unstitch part of one side where the two cloths were joined so that both American and European specialists could look underneath. Although this experiment was technically part of Riggi's program, the ever-courteous Italian allowed the Americans the privilege of first viewing.

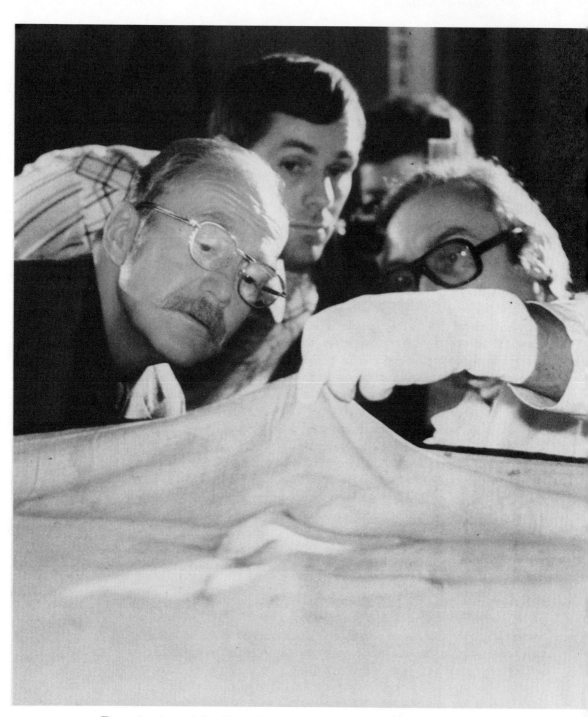

First viewing of the Shroud's underside by STURP scientists, after a portion of the backing cloth has been unstitched by Poor Clare nuns. This was the first access to the Shroud's underside in more than four centuries. *(Barrie Schwortz)*

And an important new fact was learned. While the body image exhibited not the slightest indication of any penetration to the underside, the blood image could be clearly seen to have stained right through—yet another significant difference between the two types of image. When other curiosities had been satisfied, Riggi delicately inserted his mini vacuum cleaner into the opening between the two cloths in order to suck up dust that he knew should be 450 years old.

After a grueling five days, during which key individuals such as Drs. Jackson and Jumper rarely had more than four hours sleep in any one night, it was time for return to the U.S.A. Expert analysis of the body and blood images on the sticky-tape samples was a major priority, and in this regard the team was already in touch with one of the U.S.A.'s best known microanalysts, Dr. Walter McCrone of McCrone Associates, Chicago. No stranger to problems of authenticating ancient artifacts, in 1974 McCrone had captured world headlines by showing Yale University's prized Vinland Map, purportedly a fourteenth-century (pre-Columbus) map showing America, to have been drawn by someone using an ink containing anatase, a synthesized pigment which McCrone claimed had not been developed until 1920. Shortly before the actual testing, McCrone, encouraged by an Italian royalist sympathizer, had made a unilateral and diplomatically unwise approach to ex-king Umberto of Italy regarding carbon dating. The move did not endear him to John Jackson and his colleagues and was responsible for his pointed exclusion from working directly on the Shroud in Turin. Nonetheless, late in 1978 Dr. Ray Rogers delivered the sticky-tape samples to McCrone's Chicago laboratory, where the microanalyst, a workaholic, began studying them on Christmas Day 1978, remarking in his research notebook:

> This seems to be an appropriate date to start . . . My objective is to find out what the image is. It is visible, therefore it has atoms, and we should be able to analyze those atoms. This will tell us what makes up the image and perhaps how it got there. Most likely it will turn out to be body fluids yellowed with age. It is well known that almost any organic fluids darken with time (varnish on paintings, for example). Underarm perspiration also obviously yellows cloth . . .

It was a curious preamble for an apparent personal memorandum, but if these were McCrone's expectations, they were swiftly to undergo change.

Using his favorite instrument, the conventional light micro-scope, he began taking an immediate interest in the blood-image red incrustations, remarking, ". . . too red! I've never seen dried blood look like this." By January 2, he was beginning to come close to an identification:

> Took a good look at the red particles on 3CB [blood image, chest wound area—I.W.] . . . They have very high refractive indices (very high)—very tiny, submicrometer and very deep red . . . the only possibilities are vermilion and hematite [iron oxide—I.W.] . . .

Two months later, in his notebook entry of March 3, 1979, he had become emphatic.

> I carefully examined sample 3EF [blood image, wrist wound—I.W.] and found many clumps of Fe_2O_3 hematite [color plate 12] . . . We should prepare ourselves for a negative finding re The Shroud.

Iron oxide, chemically Fe_2O_3, is nothing other than rust and is a most commonly occurring substance, to be found in virtually all dust anywhere in the world. But it has also been used as an art-ist's pigment since caveman days, and in many respects suits very well some of the hitherto puzzling properties of the Shroud's im-age. While it has often been argued that if the Shroud was the work of an artist the paint would have run from the heat of the 1532 fire, or been dissolved by the water used to quench it, unde-niably iron oxide has excellent heat resistance and it can be dis-solved only in hot concentrated acids. It is also unaffected by light.

Aware that if the Shroud iron oxide had been applied as a paint it would have to have been mixed with some form of gluey bind-ing agent, McCrone deployed a test common in painting analysis: staining samples with amido black to check if this would prove positive for proteins likely to be present in any binding medium. To his satisfaction, the test proved positive. The deduction seemed obvious that the Shroud's image must have been produced from natural, uncontaminated iron oxide that had at one time been in powdered form in a bottle or similar container, then mixed with a very dilute solution of gelatin. Inescapably the im-age was the work of an artist. Reinforcing this interpretation, McCrone found scattered among his samples stray particles of mercuric sulfide (artists' vermilion), also ultramarine and the artists' yellow pigment orpiment. The Shroud had undoubtedly been in an artist's studio.

During meetings in 1979, McCrone explained his findings to increasingly hostile members of the STURP team, who complained bitterly that he had leapt to conclusions before taking proper account of their quite contradictory findings. The following year, to a theoretically closed meeting of the British Society for the Turin Shroud and to a scientific gathering in Cardiff, he made his results increasingly public, followed, at the end of the year, by formal detailed explanations of his conclusions in his own company scientific journal *The Microscope*. Convinced by McCrone, the U.S.-born Reverend David Sox resigned as secretary of the British Society for the Turin Shroud amid a brouhaha of publicity. Much public interest in the Shroud fell away as a result of the same publicity. And although McCrone to this day acknowledges that he cannot *prove* the Shroud to be the work of an artist, he nonetheless states that he stakes his reputation that this is the case, and that any carbon dating of the Shroud will show it to be of the fourteenth century. In his own words:

I am no Don Quixote and I do not knowingly tilt at windmills. When I "tilt" I have good reasons for doing so, and in this case, I assure you, I have compelling, rational and straightforward reasons for saying the "shroud" of Turin was painted with a thin water-color paint by an artist.

So, was Bishop d'Arcis of Troyes, who condemned the Shroud as the work of an artist way back in the fourteenth century, right all the time?

If the Shroud is a forgery, could the great Leonardo da Vinci have
been its originator? Leonardo's self-portrait, c. 1512, preserved in the
Royal Library, Turin. *(Scala/Art Resource, New York)*

5

THE CASE FOR THE SHROUD IMAGE BEING THE WORK OF AN ARTIST

Some writers favorable to the authenticity of the Shroud have tried to portray Dr. Walter McCrone as a lone, heavily outnumbered maverick. But if he is wrong (and as yet this is by no means clear), nonetheless he most certainly cannot be dismissed quite so easily. A microanalyst of very considerable reputation, he lectures to the Courtauld Institute of Art in London and is widely respected in the world of art-gallery and museum scientific laboratories, which quite frequently call on his assistance in investigating possible forgeries. His *Particle Atlas*, to which he referred in identifying the Shroud particles as iron oxide, is one of the standard reference books in the specialist field of microanalysis. His painstaking researches on the Yale University Vinland Map have been widely acclaimed as of the highest analytical standards, and although those who know him well sometimes criticize his enthusiasm for self-publicity, in a personal acquaintance of some eleven years standing, and a lively correspondence, he has never given me cause for anything but respect for his competence and integrity. In combination with the already considerable historical documentation suggestive that the Shroud is the work of a fourteenth-century artist, McCrone's support for this interpretation *has* to be taken seriously. The questions therefore to be answered in this chapter are, If the Shroud *was* created by an artist, how was it done, and by whom?

With regard to the already discussed evidence that the Shroud linen is of Near Eastern derivation (as suggested particularly by Dr. Max Frei's pollen), there is no difficulty equating this with Dr. McCrone's arguments. Trade in textiles was well developed between East and West during the Middle Ages, and Geoffrey I de Charny, first certain owner of the Shroud, is known to have

65

traveled at least as far as Smyrna, the present-day Izmir, where he fought against the emir Altologo in 1346. He could easily at this time have purchased the Shroud as a plain length of linen, or acquired it among the spoils of war, the cloth perhaps having been manufactured in Palestine and carried by trading caravan across Anatolia to entrap the distinctive pollens identified by Dr. Max Frei. It is even arguable that Geoffrey de Charny may have procured a genuinely ancient cloth by this means. As McCrone has pointed out, even if the Shroud itself eventually becomes scientifically dated to the first century A.D., this is no proof that the image was not subsequently painted on by a fourteenth-century artist. The crucial factor, when considering the Shroud as the work of an artist, is determining who of all the painters of history might have been capable of producing an image of such subtlety, and how he might have set about it.

Even before McCrone published his findings, all manner of theories had been put forward. One suggestion was that a medieval artist used an actual human corpse, perhaps even crucifying this to obtain the correct blood images. In the light of the McCrone evidence, arguably such a cadaver could have been coated with a gelatin-bound iron-oxide dust to create the visible image.

This idea is perhaps the least acceptable. Use of corpses for experiment or dissection was expressly forbidden by the Church during the Middle Ages, and special permission had to be given in the case of the rare exceptions to this. More pertinently, numerous modern experiments have indicated that ordinary contact impressions of a body on cloth, whatever pigment this is coated with, fail to produce the delicate gradations of tone that are so fundamental a feature of the Shroud image.

Another popular concept has been that, instead of a body, a life-size statue or relief was employed. Prior to 1978 there was considerable interest in the Shroud body image's similarity to the scorches from the 1532 fire. It was theorized that someone in the Middle Ages had produced the Shroud's delicate gradations by wrapping the cloth around a heated metal statue, the linen receiving scorches proportionately more intense according to the cloth's distance from any one part of the hot statue. Cogent as this idea might seem, in the light of the 1978 testing it has attracted enthusiasm from neither the STURP team nor Dr. McCrone. According to STURP members, scorches fluoresce under ultraviolet light, and while the Shroud's scorches from the 1532 fire indeed do so, the body image does not. For McCrone, the consideration of a scorch does not arise, because he explains the Shroud image as due to iron oxide. In an attempt to reconcile McCrone's find-

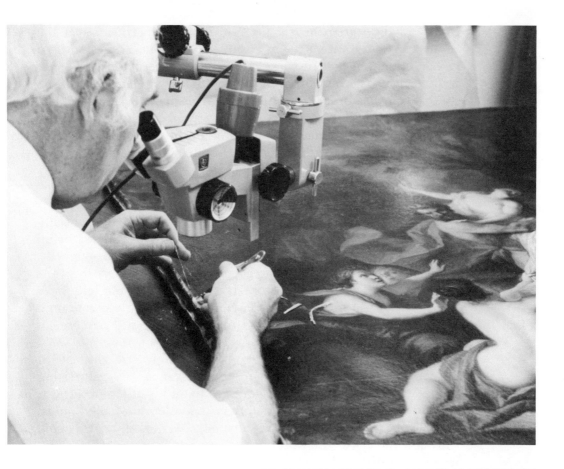

Above: Dr. Walter McCrone taking microscopic paint sample from "Titian" of very doubtful authenticity, with (right) greatly magnified Shroud fibril from area of apparent bloodstain at the right foot. Staining of this with a blue dye established the presence of protein and revealed, according to Dr. McCrone, many hundreds of tiny particles of iron oxide bound together in a sticky gelatin, evidence, in his view, that the Shroud image is the work of an artist. *(Dr. Walter McCrone)*

ings and the statue theory, Joe Nickell, an experimenter at the University of Kentucky, has produced what he argues to be a good simulation by pressing a hot-water-soaked cloth over a bas-relief statue, then daubing on an iron-oxide pigment. According to Nickell, his process produces "a true negative image." The image will be a delicate sepia in tone; it will appear to have been created without "pigment" and show no brush marks; the stain will not penetrate the fibers of the cloth but will remain a "purely surface phenomenon"—all these characteristics theoretically matching the body image on the Shroud.

But, according to McCrone, even this theory and others like it are really quite unnecessary. He regards the Shroud as essentially a conventional painting, its lack of apparent brush marks being merely because the artist used a lot of water to apply his pigment. He fails to be impressed by the negativity characteristics, dismissing these as deriving from the way an artist might have thought out the sort of contact points a body would create on a cloth wrapping. He regards the three-dimensionality as mere coincidence.

McCrone's approach is, then, a refreshingly straightforward one. But can it be sustained? It is, for instance, very surprising that some unknown artist, in addition to all his other cleverness, should have displayed the subtlety and depth of anatomical knowledge displayed on the Shroud. No amount of poring through the art of the Middle Ages reveals anyone who worked even remotely in this way.

For this reason, some of those who believe the Shroud image to be the work of an artist have been attracted to the idea that despite the apparently corroborative evidence of Bishop d'Arcis, it may be the very dating to the fourteenth century that is in error. Even prior to McCrone's analyses, this was a view put forward by Noemi Gabrielli, former director of the art galleries of Piedmont, Italy, and one of the commission appointed by Cardinal Pellegrino to examine the Shroud in 1973. According to Gabrielli in the Commission's Report:

> If we consider the [Shroud's] stylistic characteristics we must admit that this is not the same Shroud which appeared for the first time in 1356, which belonged to Count Geoffrey de Charny, and then became the property of the Dukes of Savoy. *It would appear to be a later version by about 150 years,* but still predating the fire of 1532.

Put simply, Gabrielli's argument is that sometime during the late-fifteenth century the Savoy family surreptitiously replaced an earlier, crude De Charny shroud with one created by "a great artist of the late 15th/early 16th century," this substitute being the Shroud we know today. According to Gabrielli there is not even much mystery who the "great artist" was:

> If we compare the Shroud with the face of Christ in *The Last Supper* we find a similarity in the technique and spirituality.

For Gabrielli the artist of the Turin Shroud was either the great Leonardo da Vinci himself or at least one of his school.

The idea is not as farfetched as it might at first appear. Both Leonardo da Vinci and his contemporary Michelangelo are known to have taken some delight in producing clever counterfeits, Michelangelo faking antique sculpture, Leonardo's known speciality being "dragons." If any artist may be said to be equal to the Shroud's apparent anatomical expertise, that artist must be Leonardo. As no one before him, Leonardo endlessly studied and dissected dead bodies, both animal and human. By his time, the legal restrictions on such practices had been eased, and he seems to have had the rare quality of being able to immunize himself from the obvious stench. He is one of the few artists who would quite automatically have gone to the trouble of studying the contact points a body might make on cloth, calculating the effects of gravity on blood flows and working out the exact fall of the strokes of a scourge. He is one of the few artists who would have experimented with materials to produce the subtle iron-oxide/gelatin medium identified by McCrone. He is the only artist before the nineteenth century to have used a *sfumato*, or smoky, style of painting with something of the outlineless quality of the Shroud. Above all, more than that of any other artist, only Leonardo's work exhibits significant parallels to some of the Shroud's most enigmatic features, such as the absence of apparent brush marks and of any obvious substance. As remarked of X-ray analyses of Leonardo's paintings by Madeleine Hours, director of the Louvre scientific laboratory,

> Photographs of details . . . *do not enable the brushwork or the direction of the strokes to be traced.* Examination under the microscope reveals the master's use of subtle lakes in suspension in a smooth, transparent binder, the physical structure evanesces under the various kinds of ray . . . submitted to X-rays . . . *the works reveal nothing of their structure.*

The idea, then, that Leonardo might have painted the Shroud is not without its merits. If he was indeed responsible, he must have produced it before 1516, since the distinctive poker holes already noted can be seen on a Shroud copy made in that year.

The theory does of course demand that someone from the Savoy family must secretly have commissioned Leonardo for the task, but this is by no means unthinkable in the notoriously unscrupulous times of the Renaissance. Descended from St. Louis, who acquired the alleged Crown of Thorns for Paris' Sainte Chapelle, the Savoys were politically at a low ebb in the late-fifteenth to early-sixteenth centuries, and they may well have sought a sacred status symbol like that of their ancestor in order to rally their fortunes. Was it entirely accidental that they gave the name Sainte Chapelle to the Chambéry edifice they built to house the Shroud? Could it have been mere forgetfulness that persuaded worldly Pope Julius II to overlook all forgery accusations and grant the Shroud full relic status in the year 1506? While there are no known documents suggesting the Savoys had secret dealings with Leonardo, the idea is by no means impossible. A few years ago, Maria José, widow of the late ex-king Umberto of Savoy, is known to have scoured the archives kept at her husband's Portugal retreat in order to write an as yet unpublished history of the Savoy family. According to one who has read the manuscript, Maria José dismisses the Shroud's authenticity in a single footnote, occasioning Shroud writer David Sox to remark, "One cannot help but wonder what led her to this conclusion."

While the Leonardo theory is, then, not an unattractive one, even so McCrone sees no need to support it or to date the Shroud any earlier or later than the period to which the D'Arcis document assigns it; i.e., the fourteenth century. As he points out, fine-grain iron oxide has been used by artists since prehistoric times. Italian artist Cennino Cennini of the fourteenth century certainly knew of it, referring to it as *amatito*, or hematite, and giving detailed instructions for grinding it. In the Middle Ages the best hematite was said to resemble "the color of congealed blood"—inspiration enough for a forger—and even with regard to technique the Shroud is perfectly compatible with the methods of the fourteenth century. McCrone has quoted Victorian art collector Sir Charles Eastlake on German and English techniques of painting with extreme transparency on cloth, known to have been employed in the fourteenth century. In Eastlake's words:

> In the Treviso record, preserved by Guid' Antonio Zanetti, mention is made of a German mode of painting (in watercolours) on cloth. This branch of art seems to have been practised on a large scale in England during the fourteenth century, so as to attract the notice of foreigners . . . after this

linen is painted, its thinness is no more obscured than if it was not painted at all, as the colours have no body.

For McCrone, then, there is no difficulty identifying the Shroud with the cloth so controversially exhibited by the De Charnys at Lirey. If there is relevance to the English and German cloth-painting techniques mentioned by Eastlake, it is at least noteworthy that Geoffrey de Charny was in England as a prisoner between 1349 and 1351. As a man of high rank, he may well have been allowed visits by traders and others, and undeniably it was specifically after his return from England that there were the first signs of his possession of the Shroud, in the form of his decision to build the Lirey church where it would be displayed. That the De Charny shroud was one and the same as the Shroud we know today is strongly indicated by the already discussed fourteenth-century pilgrim's medallion of a De Charny shroud exposition, in which unusual present-day Shroud features such as the small-of-the-back bloodstain seem to be readily apparent. Above all, there is the so cogent testimony of the fourteenth-century Troyes bishop D'Arcis that the De Charnys' shroud was nothing more than a clever painting of the time, "a work of human skill and not miraculously wrought or bestowed." This accords perfectly with the fourteenth century's already high reputation for forgery of relics. Could the Shroud have been, then, the work of a fourteenth-century forger? In this context, some popular misconceptions of that century's competence and attitudes need to be set to rights.

It has often been said, for instance, that an entirely nude Christ, as represented on the Shroud, would have been quite unthinkable in the mid-fourteenth century. Yet the Holkham Bible Picture Book, an English manuscript of the early-fourteenth century, has particularly gruesome representations of an entirely naked Christ being scourged and crucified, and there are similar scenes of the burial of Jesus from as early as the twelfth century. A chance reference in the *Chronicon de Melsa*, the chronicle of the English abbey of Meaux, 140 kilometers from Troyes, written about the year 1340 (directly contemporary with Geoffrey de Charny), significantly describes an abbey sculptor as having carved a wonderful crucifix by studying a nude model, a now lost piece of work which attracted wide attention at the time. Although it is true that, throughout the history of Christian art, propriety has tended to ensure a loincloth in artistic representations of Jesus' crucifixion and death, a fourteenth-century all-nude Christ is by no means impossible.

Similarly it has to be said that if there was any period that had a particular fascination for the more lurid physical aspects of the passion of Jesus, that period was the fourteenth century. Since St. Francis of Assisi, a century earlier, there had arisen a glut of visionaries and stigmatics, attracting wide attention to themselves by relivings of the Passion, and by manifesting on their bodies, seemingly as a result of an intriguing psychological condition, wounds purporting to be those of Jesus' crucifixion. Twice in her *Revelations,* St. Bridget of Sweden, directly contemporary with Geoffrey de Charny, described Jesus as having been nailed through hands and feet "where the bone was more solid"—suggestive of the Shroud wrist and ankle nailing. She also described Jesus as having been entirely naked during the scourging. Most pertinent of all, in the Papal Jubilee Year of 1350, pilgrims flocked to Rome to see special expositions of the Veronica, a cloth reputedly imprinted with sweat and blood wiped from Jesus' face as he carried his cross along the Via Dolorosa. During the expositions, a beautiful Byzantine canopy was held over the Veronica. This showed Jesus laid out in death in the identical manner of the Shroud, and could have been the very source of inspiration for the hypothetical artist who created the Shroud image. All the appropriate thinking for creating a Shroud image was undeniably in the air in the fourteenth century.

Furthermore, there is one medieval sidelight that may offer an additional insight to the Shroud's creation, if indeed the relic is the work of an artist. From the tenth century on, generally inspired by the accounts of pilgrims who had visited the Holy Sepulchre and other holy places in Jerusalem, churches of Western Europe often began to feature their own "holy sepulchre," a special structure sometimes in a side chapel, sometimes in an underground portion of the church, sometimes a portable coffin-like box. The purpose of these "sepulchres" was for dramatic Good Friday reenactments of the Passion and entombment, initially mere symbolic "burials" of a cloth-wrapped crucifix, but increasingly elaborate as the Middle Ages wore on. In place of the crucifix, there began to appear special wood sculptured figures of the dead Jesus, painted in lifelike colors and complete with realistic wounds. Although the Reformation caused most such figures to be destroyed, the Swiss Landesmuseum in Zurich has a fascinating collection of surviving examples, some of which feature the hands laid over the body in an identical manner to that of the Turin Shroud. A particularly pertinent feature of these figures is that, during the Good Friday Mass, one would be laid in the "sepulchre" wrapped in a realistic "shroud," sometimes the church's altar cloth. Between Good Friday and Easter Sunday

Early-fifteenth-century wooden sculpture of Christ figure, as used in medieval Easter sepulchre dramas, from Lucerne, Switzerland. Height 39 inches. Note the hands crossed in an identical position to those on the Shroud. *(Ian Wilson)*

Christ figure laid in "tomb," as in the Easter sepulchre dramas. In the original ceremony, the figure would have been covered with a symbolic "shroud." *(Ian Wilson)*

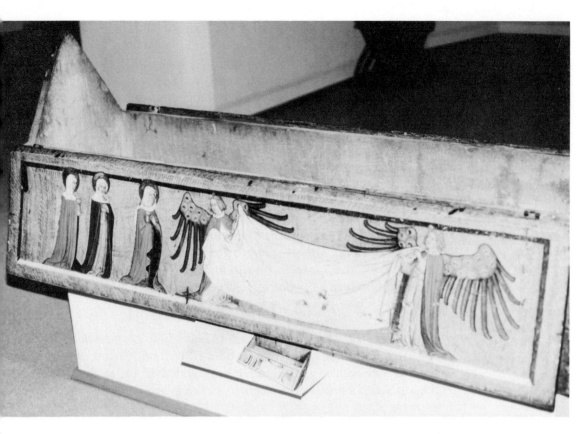

Above: Painted "tomb" as used in Easter sepulchre dramas from Baar, Canton of Zug, in Switzerland. Length 67 inches, breadth 18 inches, height 30 inches. Note the scene of a large shroud being held up to the three Marys, the very scene enacted during the Easter ceremonies. *(Ian Wilson)*

Right: Twelfth-century manuscript illustration of the three Marys visiting the empty tomb. For the association of this scene with a shroud-like Christ figure, see the full page from the manuscript reproduced on p. 115. *(Pray mss., Fol. 27v., Budapest)*

morning, the figure would be quietly removed, leaving just the "shroud," at which point the scene would be set for a powerful mini drama. At Easter Sunday morning Mass, one or two priests, appropriately costumed, would stand at the "sepulchre" in the role of the angel or angels said to have guarded Jesus' tomb. Three other priests, in different attire and carrying incense, would approach the sepulchre in the role of the three Marys.

A challenge would ring out from the "angels": "Whom do you seek in the sepulchre, O Christians?"

The Marys would answer, "Jesus of Nazareth who was crucified."

To this the angels would respond, "He is not here. He has risen even as he said before. Go proclaim he has risen from the grave."

The Marys would then go into the sepulchre, see that it was empty save for the "shroud," and emerge holding up this shroud to the congregation as proof of Jesus' resurrection. As the surviving "stage directions" of the time specifically instruct:

And when they have seen this let them . . . *take the cloth, and hold it up in the face of the clergy,* and as if to demonstrate that the Lord has risen and is no longer wrapped therein let them sing the anthem "The Lord is risen from the grave," and *lay the cloth upon the altar.*

The obvious key interest to such a drama lies in what this "shroud" cloth might have looked like. Although the ceremony would have taken different forms in different churches, there can be no doubt that in some, the "shroud" was of a very substantial size, as illustrated by an early-sixteenth-century box sepulchre from Zug, in Switzerland, showing the three Marys having held up to them a cloth incontrovertibly of Turin Shroud dimensions (see previous page). While this Zug "shroud" features no imprint, the already mentioned topicality of the Veronica story may well have inspired other churches to commission "shrouds" with imprints, to be thought out precisely in terms of the sort of impression a crucified human body would have made on a full-length cloth. In this manner, something very like the Turin Shroud could have been created by an artist without the slightest fraudulent intent, the artist's concern being solely to represent the Passion drama in the cloth's stains in the most graphic and instructive form. Such an intention for the Shroud might even explain the mysterious seamed side strip on the cloth, possibly the vestiges of a strengthening for displaying the cloth lengthwise from a long pole. And arguably Geoffrey de Charny might have obtained such a cloth in all innocence for his church, never intending that it should be regarded as anything more than a mere representation of Christ's shroud.

Whatever the facts are, undeniably this scenario has much to commend it. It would, for instance, make sense of the otherwise puzzling feature that during Geoffrey's lifetime several minor relics are listed as preserved in his Lirey church, but not the Shroud. If it was a mere stage prop, we would not expect it to have been listed. Similarly it would make sense of the already acknowledged fact that during their lifetimes Geoffrey II de Charny and Margaret de Charny referred to the Shroud only as a "likeness or representation" of the true shroud of Jesus. Presumably they, too, recognized it as a stage prop, although their actions suggest otherwise. Conceivably, the only individuals who acted fraudulently were the clergy of Lirey, trying to pass off the Shroud as the genuine article in order to attract a trade in pilgrimages. They would certainly have had every motive for this in the face of the financial ruin that threatened their patron's family after Geoffrey I de Charny's abrupt demise in 1356. Supportive of this view is the fact that Bishop d'Arcis' accusations of fraudulence are squarely leveled at the Lirey clergy rather than at the De Charnys.

Having raised such a possibility, this is perhaps an appropriate point to discuss one peculiar facet to the whole tangled and contradictory series of circumstances surrounding the Shroud's history during the fourteenth and fifteenth centuries. Despite what was a far more credulous era than our own, it is apparent that many of the earliest outsiders who viewed the Shroud at this time took a far more skeptical view of it than some quite hard-headed scientists of today. Obviously unimpressed were the two Troyes bishops, Pierre d'Arcis and Henry of Poitiers, who unhesitatingly called the Shroud "cunningly painted," condemning it as a forgery in the very earliest years after its inception. Equally unimpressed nearly a century later was Benedictine priest Cornelius Zantiflet. In 1449, Zantiflet watched the elderly Margaret de Charny exhibit the Shroud at Liège, in Belgium, and dismissed what he saw as no more than

> . . . a certain sheet on which the shape of the body of our Lord Jesus Christ has been skilfully painted with remarkable artistry . . .

Is it not strange, therefore, that little more than fifty years after Zantiflet's comment, and without any obvious resolution of the forgery charges, Pope Julius II, at the behest of the Duke of Savoy, granted the Shroud official status as one of the holiest relics of Christendom, complete with its own feast day? The day chosen for the feast was May 4, immediately after that of the discovery of the True Cross. What could have happened so decisively to change attitudes?

One possible explanation is the sheer snob appeal of the Shroud's being acquired by an illustrious family. While the De Charnys were arguably too low in the social order for anyone to believe they might possess a genuine relic, matters were altogether different for the Savoys and their grand though substanceless claims to the title of kings of Jerusalem.

Another explanation, one suggested earlier, is that a crude De Charny shroud might have been replaced by the cleverer Leonardo da Vinci-type Shroud of today. The later fifteenth century was notorious for its corruption, with Borgias occupying the Papacy, prepared to agree to anything that might enhance their influence and enrich their coffers.

A third possibility is perhaps the most intriguing of all. As we have already remarked, the Shroud mysteriously bears four sets of triple holes, which have the appearance of the cloth's having been run through three times with a red-hot poker. An unmistakable feature of this damage is that it looks deliberate—the holes occur in the dead center of the arrangement by which the cloth must have been folded at the time—and STURP's Dr. Ray Rogers has noted what appears to be pitch in close association with the damage.

No one knows when the damage occurred, except that it must have been before 1516, because the marks appear in a painted copy of that year, but it was a favorite medieval practice to use pitch-soaked pokers and the like as "trial by fire" truth devices. Accordingly, of no little interest to the mystery is a statement by French aristocrat Antoine de Lalaing relating to an exposition of the Shroud he observed at Bourg-en-Bresse on the Good Friday of the year 1503. After describing the image on the Shroud "stained with the most precious blood of Jesus, our Saviour," Lalaing went on to say that the Shroud had been

. . . boiled in oil, *tried [boute] by fire* and steamed many times, without either effacing or altering the said imprint and figure.

Now unfortunately, Lalaing did not say when the incident occurred, and his reference to such boiling in oil has always been regarded with some skepticism in view of the blackening this

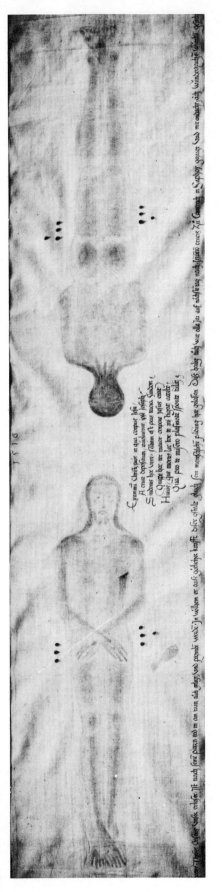

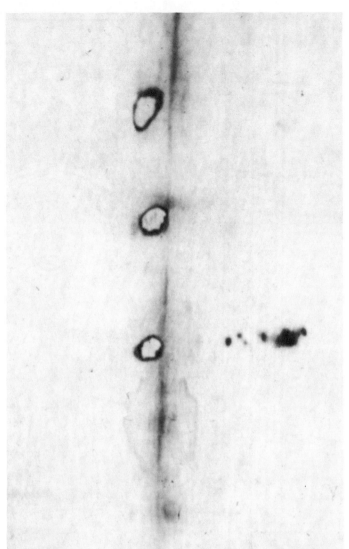

Top right: Detail of one of the sets of triple holes, as visible on the present-day Shroud. The marked blackening of the edges may denote the presence of pitch. *(Vernon Miller)*

Left: Shroud copy of 1516, from the church of St. Gommaire, Lierre, Belgium, showing the four sets of triple holes antedating the damage from the 1532 fire. If the Shroud is folded quarter-wise, the holes can be seen to coincide with the dead center of this arrangement, strongly suggesting that something like a red-hot poker was deliberately plunged into the cloth three times. *(Ian Wilson)*

Geoffrey II de Charny, drawing from a now destroyed tombstone at Froidmont. *(Bibliothèque Nationale)*

would almost certainly have caused, of which the Shroud shows no sign. But what his information does suggest is that some form of testing was carried out on the Shroud not long before the year 1503, possibly as a legally required preliminary to the institution of the full Holy Shroud cult in 1506. It further suggests that even though the image may not have been altered or effaced by the process, some form of change to the Shroud's appearance may well have occurred.

Exactly what might have happened could lie at the heart of the whole mystery of the Shroud's image. A recent BBC QED program has tried initiating some intensive experiments to reconstruct this. According to a theory evolved in this program, at the time the Shroud was first made—i.e., back in the era of the De Charnys—its image was a relatively conventional painting in light pigment on unbleached linen, which is biscuit brown in color. On application of the pigment, the linen's cellulose darkened in these areas.

There then occurred, probably in the late-fifteenth to very-early-sixteenth centuries, the "trial by fire" involving the poker incident (effectively a primitive "carbon 14" test), and, if we are to believe Lalaing's description, some form of boiling or steaming. If this was not enough, in 1532 there followed the fire at Chambéry, during which the melting of the casket and the scorching of the linen denote the subjection of the Shroud to some very high temperatures. Arguably in one or other of these incidents the Shroud's linen became bleached to its present pale yellow, most of the original painting disappeared, and what was left was a vastly more convincing-looking under stain: i.e., the image visible today. The QED program has featured replications of this process by textile specialists of Manchester's Shirley Institute and has found ready compatibility even with STURP's version of the results with the findings from the 1978 testing.

If the Shroud really is the work of an artist, then how it came into being almost certainly lies somewhere among all these alternative scenarios. But it also has to be pointed out that no scenario is entirely without its flaws and problems.

If, for instance, Geoffrey II de Charny really believed the cloth he was exhibiting was no more than an image or representation of the sort used in the annual Easter Sepulchre ceremony, why did he go to the elaborate lengths Bishop d'Arcis accuses him of in presenting the cloth with all the ritual and ceremonial of a true relic? Why did he appeal so vigorously against his local bishop's attempts to stop the expositions? And why did the Pope of the time align himself not with Bishop d'Arcis but with Geoffrey II de Charny, D'Arcis' concern to protect his see from fraudulent relicry being rewarded with a curt demand for "perpetual silence" on the matter? There seems peculiarly to have been more to the affair than any of the documents tell us.

A further difficulty is one of determining, if we are dealing with an artist of the time of the De Charnys, who that artist might have been. A tempting possibility is that it might have been the same English abbey artist who sculptured the earlier-mentioned Meaux crucifix, perhaps an obscure Leonardo da Vinci of his time. If this is so, no independent trace of him has survived, but the idea that there might have been such a man cannot be entirely discounted. Virtually everything of Meaux as it existed in the time of Geoffrey de Charny was destroyed in the suppression of the Jacquerie uprising of 1358. This imponderable aside, the Shroud, certainly as it appears today, has no similarity to the work of any known artist either of the Gothic period or any other time, and with the single exception of Gabrielli and her Leonardo da Vinci hypothesis, no present-day art expert has come forward to make a serious attribution of this kind.

All that can be said is that if the Shroud is the work of an artist, whoever he was and wherever he worked, his approach to the task was one of the most remarkable skill and inventiveness. If, for instance, as McCrone has suggested, he simply thought out the Shroud's negativity as a pattern of contact points, his subtlety and accuracy with no means of checking his work is well-nigh incredible. His differentness is quite clear from scrutiny of the artists' copies that have since been made of the Shroud, not one of which manages to look anything but the work of a human hand.

A similar comparison with conventional artists' works is worthwhile in respect of the Shroud's scourge marks and blood flows. Plenty of artists have depicted Jesus being savagely scourged, his body covered with wounds. But not one has tried to think out a patterning as complex as that on the Shroud, the fanning out of the scourge's thongs, the paired fall of the pellets; not one has depicted wounds with such gravitational logic or such a convincingly trickled appearance.

A further difficulty in terms of the actual execution of the Shroud is how, unless the original appearance has been considerably altered along the lines of the QED hypothesis, the artist was able to see what he was doing when creating the Shroud image. If working up close, he would have had the greatest difficulty seeing the overall effect he was creating. If working at a distance, he would have needed something like a twelve-foot paintbrush!

Even if the Shroud is the work of an artist, there are, then, considerable difficulties understanding this and setting it in a proper historical context. Because there are these difficulties, and since the McCrone viewpoint is fiercely disputed by other scientists, it is only right that we should now consider equally objectively the alternative viewpoint: that the Shroud image is genuinely of some spontaneous, nonhuman causation, and potentially nearly two thousand years old.

Drs. Heller and Adler at work on Shroud samples. *(Vernon Miller)*

6

THE CASE FOR THE SHROUD IMAGE *NOT* BEING THE WORK OF AN ARTIST

Those who dismiss the Shroud as the work of an artist often accuse the STURP team of having been an overly religious group so committed to the idea of the Shroud's genuineness that they have blinded themselves to any evidence to the contrary. Such a view is equally as unfair as uncharitable attitudes toward Dr. Walter McCrone. A census of the religious affiliations of the Shroud team conducted by Tom D'Muhala revealed six agnostics, two Mormons, three Jews, four Catholics, with the rest varying colors of Protestant: Methodist, Lutheran, Congregationalist, Baptist, Presbyterian, Episcopalian, and Dutch Reformed. While it would be true to say that certain key individuals such as Dr. John Jackson are deeply religious, the chemical evidence on which much of this chapter is based happens to derive principally from a non-practicing Jew, Dr. Alan Adler. And for a staunch Episcopalian such as the thermal chemist Dr. Ray Rogers, the attitude even before setting foot in Turin was one of objective scientific skepticism:

> I really was about 50% sure we'd walk in, spend thirty minutes looking at it, and decide it was hoaxed . . . not worth doing our tests on . . .

Such an attitude is in fact implicit even from the very tests the STURP team incorporated from the very outset into their program. X-ray fluorescence analysis, ultraviolet spectrophotometry, visible reflectance spectroscopy, and infrared spectroscopy—all

85

are scientific methods of gathering data for the identification of a compound such as an artist's pigment. Had an art-gallery scientific laboratory been called in to analyze the Shroud specifically as the work of some unknown artist, they would have used much the same methodology. And it is in fact precisely because they worked in such a wide-ranging manner that, almost to a man, both the original STURP team and those whose expertise they have called upon in the most recent years contend that McCrone has misinterpreted his data and has drawn quite the wrong conclusion.

No one is more conscious than the present author of the difficulty, for a non-scientific layman, of trying to weigh the relative merits of two bitterly opposed scientific camps, both well qualified, both arguing in complex scientific terminology.

But there are ways in which, even from simple study of photographs in this book, grounds for doubt arise concerning McCrone's justification for quite the rigid negative stance he has adopted, particularly in view of the fact that he has never had direct access to the Shroud. As I was able to observe for myself in 1973, when the Shroud's blood images are examined at close quarters, they are distinctively different, both in color and character, from what is termed the body image; that is, the stains representing arms, face, etc. The former have a subtle but readily perceptible carmine hue and remain quite distinguishable when examined up close; the latter appear simply as a variation of the already yellowish hue of the cloth itself and seem to fade almost imperceptibly into this whenever one tries to inspect them more closely (color plates 15 and 16). The fact of some significant distinction between body and blood images is confirmed by the affirmation on the part of both Europeans and Americans participating in the 1978 testing that when the underside of the Shroud was examined, the blood images showed through, while the body ones did not penetrate the cloth. And the same distinction is obvious to anyone studying the transmitted-light photographs (color plates 11 and 12), the blood images showing up strongly (indicating the presence of some definite substance), and the body images so effectively disappearing that if any substance is present, it is too thin to be on anything but the surface of the cloth.

Yet, for McCrone in his published reports, there is no qualitative distinction to be made between body and blood images, the apparent greater solidity of the latter being straightforwardly "an indication of the larger quantity of iron oxide in these areas."

While the layman might feel prepared to accept McCrone's microanalytical judgment on such a matter, the justification for

STURP scientists view the Shroud with transmitted light. *(Ernest Brooks)*

trusting that judgment dissolves on close scrutiny of the second table in McCrone's first *Microscope* paper on the Shroud, showing the relative numbers of purported iron-oxide-coated fibrils to noncoated fibrils in any one sample. Puzzlingly, this shows a sample of body image (from a finger) containing as many as 72 percent "colored" fibrils, compared to a sample of blood image (from the heel) containing as little as 42 percent. Purportedly, exact numbers of fibrils are quoted. Since on McCrone's own arguments one would expect blood image to contain more coloring than body image, I questioned him on this point in personal correspondence and received a surprisingly candid reply:

> I have to confess that those numbers aren't as precise as one would like to have them. They were obtained by looking at the individual tapes and judging whether the degree of yellow color of the fibers constituted yellowing over and above the amount present . . . even in the control areas [i.e. those areas with no image—I.W.]. It was often pretty difficult to make this decision, and for this reason the number should not be interpreted as anything like exact. They could easily vary by 20% or 30%.

Suddenly one comes face to face with the realization that Mc-Crone's seemingly precise statistics in support of his arguments are nothing of the kind. He has simply estimated numbers, understandable when the eye is trying to distinguish shades of yellow, but nonetheless unacceptably unscientific. The consequent justification for questioning his interpretations increases further when it is realized that the McCrone/STURP dispute is not about the actual presence of iron oxide, which STURP readily acknowledges is abundant on the Shroud, but (a) its precise nature in any one sample and (b) its relevance as a contributor to specific forms of the various images seen on various parts of the cloth.

Thus, as STURP scientists Morris, Schwalbe, and London showed in their X-ray fluorescence analysis, iron, along with calcium and strontium, is present in trace quantities all over the Shroud. Some of the blood image areas show a slightly stronger signal, but this is consistent with blood itself containing around 1 percent iron. One nonimage area exhibited a very high signal, identifiable with common dirt, where the man of the Shroud's feet would have been. But, as revealed by a careful scan across body image areas, these produced a signal for iron no different from that in any of the nonimage areas.

In other words, variation in iron content could not be correlated to any of the variations seen in the Shroud's body image coloration. Exactly the same deduction was evident from the absence of any observation of body and blood image in the Shroud X radiographs. Since whenever quantities of iron oxide sufficient to be visible to the human eye are daubed onto pieces of cloth, they show up under X-radiography—an experiment actually carried out by Boston physician Dr. Gilbert Lavoie—the only reasonable inference is that whatever is responsible for the Shroud body and blood images cannot be iron oxide.

It would, of course, be unfair to dismiss McCrone quite as easily as this. Even if the iron oxide is not responsible for the images, we need to know why it should be present on the Shroud in quantities sufficient for McCrone to mistake it for the image. We also need to know how, if not by an artist's iron-oxide pigment, the images may be considered to have been formed. Once the intransigence of McCrone's views was realized, the individuals invited by STURP to address themselves to these questions were physician Dr. John Heller of Connecticut's now defunct New England Institute, and more impressively, ebullient chemistry professor Dr. Alan Adler of Western Connecticut State University. Of Jewish parentage, and a noted specialist in the heme and porphyrin components of human blood, Adler became associated with the Shroud project at Heller's instigation, initially anticipating that the work might take him a mere couple of days. As time progressed, he found himself undertaking more than a thousand separate tests on the Shroud's body and blood image chemistry. As reasoned by Adler, McCrone looked down his microscope and pronounced only on the basis of optical criteria. But the only true way to understand the nature of the Shroud body and blood images is to study their chemical reactions under a variety of chemical treatments.

An obvious key feature of interest was those particles reliably identified by Dr. McCrone as iron oxide. As soon as the complete set of tape samples had been received from McCrone and Rogers, Adler scoured them for definite iron-oxide specimens that he could subject to special study.

He found that the principal areas from which they derived were the edges of the lozenge-shaped stains from the water used to douse the 1532 fire. Interestingly, it was precisely those stains, altogether more insignificant than those of the body and blood images, that *did* show up under the X radiographs. So what were particles of iron oxide doing in these regions? Every test that was applied, for birefringence (double refraction), pleochroism (transmission of different colors in different directions), etc., as well as

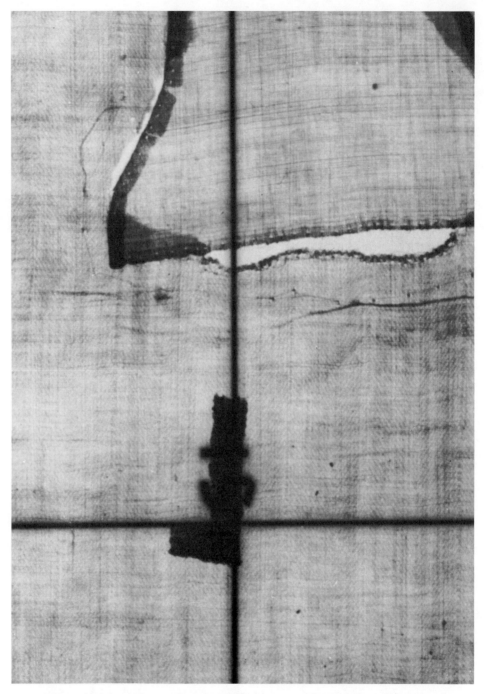

The area of the Shroud chest wound, as seen on an X-ray plate. An
analysis shows how the "blood" image fails to register under X ray,
indicating that any substance, if present, can be of only very light
atomic weight. Compare this X-radiograph with the natural-light
view of the chest wound on p. 27. *(W. Mottern)*

chemistry, confirmed that the particles were indeed iron oxide. But, as study with an electron microscope quickly revealed, there was something unusual about them. They were exceptionally pure.

Artists' pigment iron oxides from the Mediterranean, whether medieval or more recent, tend invariably to be contaminated by elements such as manganese, nickel, and cobalt. But the Shroud iron oxide was chemically pure to a level of 99+ percent. So how had it been formed? As this initially baffled both Heller and Adler, Heller began badgering museums for the loan of cloth specimens of known antiquity, obtaining in this manner a Coptic gravecloth datable to around A.D. 350, some Egyptian burial linen of the mid second millennium B.C., along with a piece of three-hundred-year-old Spanish linen owned by his wife. As Adler soon discovered, all exhibit the "chemically pure" iron, along with calcium, which the X-ray fluorescence similarly had detected on the Shroud. Why should this be so?

Extensive browsing through textbooks on how linen is produced provided the answer. Linen derives, of course, from the plant flax, which, after cutting, undergoes a series of preparations for linen making, one of which is a fermentation process called retting, involving a long period of soaking in large outdoor vats or bodies of water. There is a very strong, characteristic smell during this process, but the crucial feature is its chemistry. As everything ferments away, bar the flax's key component, its cellulose, an exchange process occurs between that cellulose and the water environment in which it finds itself. The three metals abundant in natural waters that most commonly exchange with cellulose are iron, calcium, and strontium, exactly as found on the Shroud and the other old linens. Herein lay the explanation for why the Shroud iron is so pure. It derives from an entirely natural process. As proof that this was what occurred, Heller and Adler found tiny iron-oxide "cannon-balls," sometimes inside the bamboo-like structure of the linen fibrils, where no artist could possibly have placed them. The migration of ions at the time of the 1532 fire, coupled with the heat, would have naturally produced the iron-oxide particles seen at the water-stain margins. These would then have translocated all over the cloth during the repeated folding and unrolling that occurred every time the Shroud was exhibited.

So herein lay an explanation for why McCrone found the Shroud samples so "abundant" in iron oxide, but if these were not responsible for what the eye sees as body and blood images, what was? First Heller and Adler reexamined the close-up photo-

graphs of Shroud blood image areas taken with the Wild M400
Photomakroscope. Certainly these looked like blood. The substance had cemented some of the linen fibrils together. It had
some capillarity, since the unstitching of one side of the Shroud
had revealed a soaking through to the underside. Also consistent
with blood were the variations seen in the particulate matter's
color and form. When blood clots, it separates, giving the same
sort of range of color evident on the Shroud. But such observations were no answer to McCrone; they represented merely one
subjective interpretation against another. If the Shroud blood image was to be proved to be blood, it needed to be demonstrated as
such under a variety of stringent chemical tests.

As Heller and Adler focused their attention on the slides la-
beled as from blood image areas, they realized something of the
demands of the task they had taken on. No U.S. blood specialist
had been with Jackson and his team in Turin, and the samples
removed via sticky tape were absolutely minute, in microanalytical measurement ranging from nanograms (billionths of a gram)
to at best a microgram, a millionth of a gram. Everything had to
be cut from the tapes, transferred onto spot plates on a dissecting
microscope, and treated with solvents to remove the tape adhesive
before even the most elementary chemical examination could begin.

Isolating one "blood" fibril clearly encrusted with some form of
red particles, Adler decided that he first needed to establish that
this was not simply another sample of iron oxide. As already remarked, iron oxide applied to a linen fibril has certain known
properties, such as birefringence and pleochroism, under polarization. A simple test for birefringence involves placing the specimen between two polaroids set crossed to each other, in which
iron-oxide particles show up as bright red speckles. The Shroud
particles failed to respond either for this or for pleochroism, or
for an alternative refractive-index test. They also failed to behave
chemically like iron oxide; therefore they cannot be iron oxide.

Having established what they are not, the next step was to
proceed to what they are. Several particles were found to have
broken away from their fibrils, in the manner of a replica-cast.
One specimen selected by Adler seemed to be thin enough for
microspectrophotometry, a method of identifying particles of unknown composition by analyzing their wavelength spectra. When
plotted on such a graph, every substance exhibits a pattern of
peaks and valleys as distinctive as a fingerprint. As Adler knew, if
the Shroud particle was blood, its heme/porphyrin components
should exhibit a pronounced peak, the so-called Soret band, at

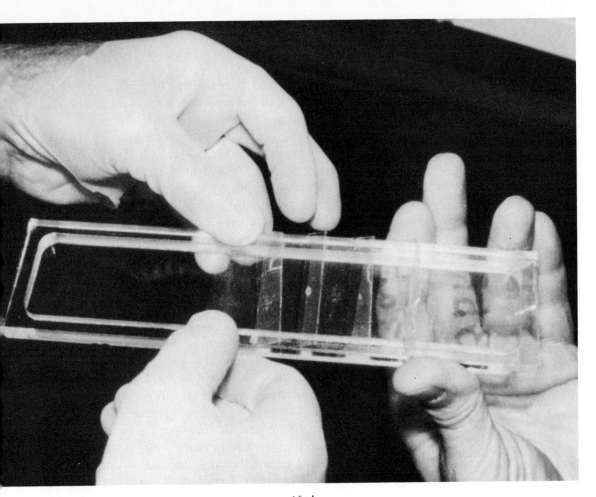

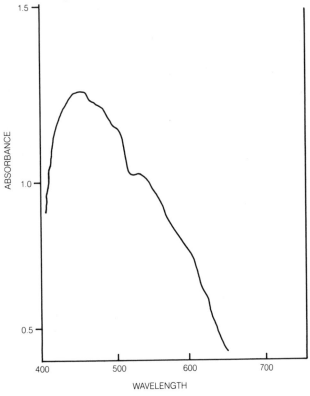

Shroud tape samples mounted ready for transport back to the United States, with (right) graph of transmission spectrum of Shroud "blood" particles as indicated by microspectrophotometer. Wavelength is in nanometers. *(Vernon Miller, Alan Adler)*

approximately 410 nanometers, thereafter falling off sharply. At Yale University, where he had been a professor of medicine and medical physics, Heller managed to beg the use of a microspectrophotometer and help from a well-known biologist, Dr. Joseph Gall. Although Gall expressed some misgivings about the less than ideal nature of the sample, he had no misgivings about the result. At 410 nanometers the sample's spectral pattern exhibited a Mount Everest of a peak, falling off sharply. When Heller showed the graph to Adler, a heme and porphyrin specialist, Adler's reaction was unequivocal. Unmistakably the particle was hemoglobin, in the acid methemoglobin form, denatured, as would be expected in a very old sample. Chemical tests then quickly confirmed the presence of porphyrin-containing materials.

Although there were some seeming anomalies to the graph's peaks and valleys, wherever Adler gave proper study to them he found a ready explanation. For instance, two minor peaks that he did not immediately recognize, he subsequently realized must represent bile pigments, such as bilirubin, which occur when blood is broken down. One test for such an interpretation was to take actual methemoglobin, bilirubin, and another detected element, albumin, and experiment with their proportions in order to simulate the Shroud spectra in laboratory conditions. A simulation was achieved. Independently the reagent Bromcromesol Green was used to test chemically for albumin, proving positive. A later immunochemical test also confirmed the presence of a primate albumin. A further test was to apply to the Shroud "blood" samples a recognized clinical test for the presence of bilirubin, proving positive.

But the surprise was the high proportion of bilirubin, far more than would be expected in a normally healthy human being. The only possible interpretation was that at the time of his death the man of the Shroud must have been severely, horribly jaundiced, with huge quantities of bile pigments present in his bloodstream. But why? Consultation with physicians provided an answer. Outside actual illness, the conditions in which such severe jaundicing can occur are severe concussive injuries, such as occur in road accidents, but which would also be consistent with the sort of severe beating and scourging which the man of the Shroud appears to have undergone. The effect of such a severe beating is to hemolyze, or disrupt many of the red blood corpuscles. When the hemoglobin so released reaches the liver, it produces bilirubin, responsible for the reddish-orange pigment in bile.

Suddenly even chemistry seemed to be contributing to the grim story of how the man of the Shroud met his death.

But, for Adler, there was one further major test requisite to any proper identification of blood: that for the presence of protein. For this there are several methods possible; one, staining with amido black, having been what McCrone used for detecting what he interpreted as the artist's gelatin binding medium. But, as found by Adler, this and similar dye methods give misleading "positive" results for any cellulose that, like the Shroud, has become oxidized. They cannot be considered determinative, and for technical reasons the popular and highly sensitive ninhydrin method also proved unsuitable. For Adler, the "gangbuster" method turned out to be using proteases. After twenty minutes of application to a Shroud "blood" fibril, the blood protein could be seen to dissolve away, not only confirming the presence of a protein, but also leaving a fibril that in its microscopic and chemical characteristics most resembled those areas of the Shroud untouched by any image. As recognized by Adler, the implication of this was that the Shroud "blood" went onto the cloth before whatever process was responsible for the body image, the very reverse of the way any artist could be expected to work.

All in all, Heller and Adler argue that the Shroud blood images are determinable as genuine blood by no less than twelve independent indications: their forensic appearance, their microscopic appearance, the microspectrophotometry, reflection spectrometry, the presence of bile pigments, the presence of protein, the presence of albumin, positive protease tests, positive hemochromogen tests, positive cyanmethemoglobin tests, chemical generation of characteristic porphyrin fluorescence, and the already mentioned X-ray fluorescence detection of slightly higher levels of iron in blood image areas. Nonetheless, before this is accepted, the layman is entitled to ask why, in contrast to the normal behavior of blood, which turns brown and flakes off, the Shroud stains exhibit such completeness and such reddishness. Some carefully researched answers to this have been provided by Boston physician Dr. Gilbert Lavoie, who has made a special study of blood-clotting and image-transfer behavior under a wide variety of conditions: differing levels of humidity, temperatures, angles at which the wound is held, etc. According to Lavoie, who notes that similar observations were made as long as eighty years ago by the French biologist Paul Vignon, the Shroud bloodstains make good sense once they are considered impressions from blood that has clotted for a certain period of time. In experimental work, he found that the best impressions derive specifically from wounds that have been held vertical (i.e., in the position obligatory in crucifixion), excess oozed serum tending to drip

off these, leaving a clotted surface with just the right gelatinous
consistency for a good impression. At least an hour's nondis-
turbance is needed for the most Shroud-like results. And this very
same process also provided Adler with the key to the Shroud
blood images' unusual reddish color. In Lavoie's reconstruction,
the red cells, the very elements familiarly known to flake off, do
not transfer to the cloth. It is the oozed serum which transfers to
the cloth, its chief constituents the brownish methemoglobin and
albumin, with which the greatly increased proportion of the reddish pigment bilirubin would have formed a natural bond.
Therein lay the explanation for the apparently misleading
"fresh" appearance and permanence of the Shroud blood images
that led many to doubt the blood images as really due to blood.

Working quite independently of Heller and Adler, across the
Atlantic in Turin, pathologist Professor Pier Baima Bollone, examining a complete blood image thread from the Shroud, likewise
concluded that this was indeed blood, the immunological tests
possible from this greater amount of sample enabling him, unlike
Heller and Adler, quite specifically to identify this blood as human and of the AB blood group. Although Bollone's claim should
be treated with caution, "primate" blood being all that can un-
equivocally be claimed, nonetheless as commented by Adler in an
address to the Chemistry Department of Queen Mary College,
University of London, in July 1984:

> The chemistry is saying the same as the forensics. There is only
> one way that this kind of chemistry could appear on the cloth.
> This cloth had to be in contact with the body of a severely
> beaten human male.

As Adler was quick to realize, however, while confirming the
blood images as genuine blood involved one battery of chemical
tests, identifying what was responsible for the Shroud body images, that is, the stains representing face, hands, etc., demanded
quite different approaches. As will be recalled from the transmitted-light photography, unlike the blood, the body images seemed
to have insufficient substance to act as any form of barrier to the
light. As also noted, even the highest magnifications with the
Wild Photomakroscope by Pellicori and Evans revealed no particles or other solid matter that might be construed as responsible
for the image, each image fibril appearing quite separate from the
next, with nothing appearing to bind it to its neighbor in the
manner of the gelatin argued for by Dr. McCrone. It was as if
there was nothing there, the only visual indication that the body

images had some difference from those without image being their straw-yellow color when seen at high magnification. This discoloration, which itself was very difficult to distinguish, affected only the very uppermost fibrils of a thread, to no more than one or two fibrils' depth. As Adler has wryly commented,

"That's an awful light touch this artist has got."

Intrigued, Adler applied test after test to body image fibrils in an endeavor to get some form of identifying reaction. Archaeological chemist Professor Max Saltzman of the University of California, Los Angeles, has produced a series of solvents spanning the entire solubility range by which the presence of any known dye, ancient or modern, synthetic or natural, can be isolated and its type determined. Not one of these had any effect on the Shroud body image. The protease tests, which had been so responsive in the blood image areas, proved consistently negative when applied to body image samples, another indication of the error of McCrone's failure to make a proper distinction between the body and blood image areas. Most strong acids also failed to change the body image color, the only substances able to bleach it proving to be hydrazine, alkaline peroxide, and diimide, all three superstrong bleaches. The substance most meaningful in respect of the body image chemistry turned out to be sulfuric acid. If this was added to a body image fibril, the fibril turned darker. If it was added to a nonimage fibril, the fibril acquired an appearance indistinguishable from the body image (color plate 18). This implied that whatever was responsible for the Shroud's body image was something strongly dehydrative and strongly oxidative; i.e., affecting the cloth in at least some manner closely akin to sulfuric acid's chemistry.

One possibility to which this gives rise, inevitably, is the idea that an artist somehow painted in sulfuric acid. One can only boggle at what use of such a medium might have done to anyone's brush, but quite aside from such considerations, Adler has pointed out one further constraint that the hypothetical artist put upon himself. As noted by Jumper, there is very little variation in coloring between one Shroud body image fibril and another, the apparent "shadings" the eye sees on the Shroud being composed simply of greater or lesser numbers of relatively identically toned image fibrils—just as light and shade on a newspaper photograph is created by greater and lesser numbers of tiny dots. As remarked by Adler,

From Dr. Volckringer's collection, the imprint of a plant collected and pressed, with (right) how this appears on a photographic negative. A remarkable parallel to the Shroud imprint, the exact process of plant image formation is still not fully understood. (*Jean Willemin, courtesy Dr. Jean Volckringer*)

This tells us something immediately. It tells us the thickness of the artist's brush. It has to be one fibril wide. That's less than the thickness of a human hair. Now he (the artist) has another problem. He has to keep track of the number of fibrils he discolors per unit area to produce the reversed image . . . it is impossible for someone to make such an artistic rendition by painting it . . .

The overall implication of the Shroud body image is, in fact, that it seems to derive not from any substance—paint or dye—having been added to the linen but, rather, from something of the linen's own substance having been taken away; in other words, an oxidation, degradation, or aging of the linen's cellulose that has for some reason been accelerated in those areas closest to the hypothetical body which the linen once wrapped. Oxidation itself is, in fact, one of the most common processes in all nature, one close analogy being the well-known yellowing of newspaper (itself a form of cellulose) when exposed to strong sunlight. But while it is easy to understand how sunlight, with its obvious dehydrative effects, can cause a generalized yellowing, or oxidation, it is altogether more difficult to find an analogy for a body, theoretically cold in a tomb, producing the same. No other known shrouds have been found to bear imprints even beginning to approach the photographic quality of the Turin specimen. There is, however, one intriguing, conceivably related parallel known from the plant kingdom.

All over the world, university botany departments and their like preserve old collections of pressed plants, and as has been very ably pointed out by a now retired French pharmacist, Dr. Jean Volckringer, the heavy paper covering these plants is not uncommonly imprinted with a striking image of the specimen involved. Some of the parallels of these to the Shroud are remarkable. They are invariably sepia in color and lack any obvious image-forming substance. They occur on the paper above and below the plant specimen and feature considerable observable detail, often every tiny vein of a leaf, very reminiscent of the almost X-ray quality of the Shroud's image of the hands. Flowers, leaves, stems and roots all leave their image with the same completeness, the process thus seeming independent of localized plant secretions such as resins, oils, chlorophyll, etc. The imprints have inverse relief characteristics; that is they become fainter the greater the distance of any one part of the plant from the cover paper, yet they reproduce, apparently without direct contact, over that distance. Above all, just like the Shroud, they become lifelike and

photographic when seen in negative, even exhibiting the same
effect of naturally lit relief and the same three-dimensionality
when viewed under a VP8 Image Analyzer. Besides these visual
similarities to the Shroud's image, which Volckringer noted as far
back as the 1940s, the important fact is that the plant images derive from an undoubted dehydration/degradation/oxidation, the
reaction in this instance occurring on the cellulose of the rag
paper in which the plant specimen has been pressed. That such a
process has been at work in at least these examples has been acknowledged even by Dr. Walter McCrone; he would simply deny
that this has occurred in the case of the Shroud. But even if the
Shroud image does derive from this plantlike process, why it
should have occurred so uniquely in the case of this one crucifixion victim continues to remain the Shroud's central mystery. And
even more strikingly than in the case of the bloodstains, it seems
to put the creation of the image beyond human artifice.

Drs. Heller and Adler's arguments have been widely published
in reputable scientific journals, and with the major exception of
Dr. Walter McCrone, their thinking and methodology have received no serious challenge. Nonetheless there is one claim of
McCrone's that we have yet to consider: his assertion that in the
course of his examinations of the Shroud fibers he found, besides
iron oxide, certain other undeniable paint pigments, notably vermilion, ultramarine, and orpiment. In fact there is, again, no
quarrel about the actuality of such particles on the Shroud. Heller
and Adler reported them also, as did the Italian microanalyst
Riggi. But as the latter three would argue, such particles are
strays, or adventitious materials, with no justification for being
considered contributory to the Shroud's actual images.

Although McCrone would reply that they at least indicate that
the Shroud has been in an artist's studio, which in itself suggests
that that artist may have been the forger, such a view fails to take
account of the Shroud's known close associations with artists
through many centuries: artists who were its copyists, not its
creators. A special study of artists' copies of the Shroud has been
made by Italian Salesian scholar Don Luigi Fossati, who shows
that among Spain's many copies of the Shroud are full-size ver-
sions in the churches of Guadalupe, Navarrete, Torres de la Ala-
meda, Logrono, La Cuesta, and Agliè, created between the years
1568 and 1822. The inscriptions on these copies state that each has
not only been copied from the original—with the artist inevitably
grinding his colors in close proximity—but also that they have,
for sanctification purposes, been placed in actual one-to-one contact with the Shroud—as on the Agliè example:

. . . laid upon the Most Holy Shroud so that the two were perfectly fitted together in every part.

Italian examples from Moncalieri, Bitonto, and Naples, dated 1634, 1646, and 1652, respectively, tell exactly the same story, and in fact the easy incidence of stray paint particles falling on the Shroud was exemplified even during the 1978 testing, paint particles from the frescoes high on the ceiling of the Turin Palace prince's suite falling on the American scientists even as they worked.

Overall, as Dr. Alan Adler would sum up the exhaustive work he and his colleagues have done on the Shroud:

By the rules of science we have not been able to *dis*authenticate this image.

This is another way of saying that science has not been able to prove the Shroud the work of human hands, and that, as we are about to see, has remarkable relevance to a reconsideration of the Shroud's early history.

Present-day Urfa, in eastern Turkey, the site of the ancient city of Edessa. Was this a home for the Shroud in earlier centuries? *(Lennox Manton)*

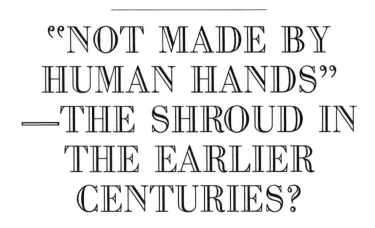

7

"NOT MADE BY HUMAN HANDS" —THE SHROUD IN THE EARLIER CENTURIES?

If the Shroud is of genuine antiquity and is not the work of an artist, how are we to understand its history before the time of the De Charnys?

As was made clear in the very first chapter, a particularly major objection to the Shroud's authenticity has always been posed by the apparently damning memorandum of the fourteenth-century Bishop d'Arcis of Troyes, combined with an apparent absence of clear references from earlier centuries to a Shroud answering the description of that preserved in Turin. Some investigators, such as the late Fr. Paul de Gail of France, have been attracted to scraps such as a Gospel of the Hebrews reference to Jesus' giving his shroud to "a servant of the High Priest." But, however tantalizing, the reference survives only as an isolated quotation from the writings of St. Jerome. Even if the cloth referred to was one and the same as the present-day Turin Shroud, the reference provides no form of peg upon which to begin a reconstruction of the Shroud's history. Although often quoted, little more satisfactory is seventh-century pilgrim Arculf's description of a supposed shroud of Jesus he saw in Jerusalem. Arculf described the cloth as only about eight feet long and made no mention of its bearing any image. As has very cogently been argued by Jesuit Fr. Francez (see bibliography), the cloth Arculf saw in Jerusalem was almost certainly a so-called holy shroud of Compiègne, destroyed in the French Revolution.

Similarly unconvincing have been attempts to explain the apparent silence as due to the destruction of early records. While

103

vast quantities of manuscript material from the Dark Ages have undoubtedly been lost to us, accounts of Christendom's relics are among the most common of the material that has survived, and had there been anywhere obvious so interesting an object as the Turin Shroud we would surely have heard of it. The only early literary reference seeming to suggest for it some prefourteenth-century existence is an account by Crusader Robert de Clari that in August 1203, shortly before the sack of Constantinople, he saw in that city a church

> . . . which they called My Lady St. Mary of Blachernae, where was kept the *sydoine* in which Our Lord was wrapped, which stood up straight every Friday so that the [figure] of Our Lord could be plainly seen there.

To this De Clari added intriguingly:

> No one, either Greek or French, ever knew what became of this *sydoine* after the city was taken.

Unfortunately, the very isolation of this reference has made it as unhelpful as it is tantalizing. Constantinople was, throughout the Dark Ages, a Fort Knox of Christian relics, the comings and goings of which were usually well recorded. The Empress Helena caused a sensation in the fourth century when she discovered in Jerusalem what she thought to be the "True Cross," the crosses of the thieves crucified with Jesus, the "crown of thorns," and the *titulus*, or title board, of Jesus' cross, all of which she brought back with her to Constantinople. In the twelfth century, Emperor Manuel I Comnenus met at the port of Constantinople a ship bearing what was believed to be the stone on which the body of Jesus was washed prior to burial, and Comnenus personally carried this on his back uptown to install it in its new home. However suspect the authenticity of such relics, and even though most subsequently became dispersed across Europe, the history of each can usually be reliably traced century by century. Yet even if the present-day Shroud was one and the same as the *sydoine* described by De Clari in Constantinople, there is no clear record of either the coming or the going of this. The question that arises is whether this makes it yet more likely that the Shroud must be the work of some fourteenth-century painter, or whether there could be some other possible explanation.

One potentially rewarding approach is to consider whether, independent of literary references, there are any visual clues to the possible early existence of the cloth we know today as the Turin Shroud. Particularly interesting in this connection are the portraits of Jesus that have come down to us through the centuries, portraits which, it is to be noted, correspond very closely with the bearded, long-haired image visible, even without the aid of the photographic negative, on the Shroud linen itself.

It needs to be recognized that while if the Shroud is the work of an artist of the fourteenth century the artist would obviously have copied the traditional likeness of the time, if, on the other hand, it genuinely derives from the first century and was subsequently preserved somewhere accessible, then inevitably early artists must have consulted it as a guide to Jesus' earthly appearance, of which there is no information provided in the Gospels. Following this line of thinking, it seems at least potentially productive to try to trace how far back the conventional Jesus likeness can be found in works of art and to try to determine whether this offers any clues that the Shroud image may lie behind it.

A study of this kind is, to say the least, illuminating. A consistent Shroud-like, long-haired, fork-bearded, front-facing likeness of Christ can be traced back through numerous works in the Byzantine tradition dating many centuries before the time of Geoffrey de Charny. Beginning with the twelfth century, there is an imposing Christ Pantocrator from Cefalù, Sicily. From about a century earlier, a similar, almost terrifying Pantocrator glowers from the dome of the church of Daphni, near Athens. From back to the tenth century, a still familiar-looking Christ Enthroned stares out from the church of St. Angelo in Formis, near Capua (color plate 21). Datable back to the eighth century, a similar-looking Christ portrait is to be found in the depths of the Pontianus catacomb, near Rome. As early as the sixth century, still with the same facial resemblance, are a Christ portrait on a silver vase found at Homs, in present-day Syria, and a beautiful icon of Christ Pantocrator from the monastery of St. Catherine in the Sinai Desert. Despite stylistic variations, each of these works seems inspired by the same tradition of Jesus' earthly appearance. And each has a strong resemblance to the face visible on the Shroud.

In this connection, as early as the 1930s a Frenchman, Paul Vignon, pointed out among this same family of Christ portraits a recurrence of certain strange markings seemingly derivative from the Shroud. One example is a starkly geometrical topless square visible between the eyebrows on the Shroud image. Exactly what this feature is remains undetermined, but it is to be seen in the identical position on the eighth-century Pontianus portrait, curi-

Christ face, eleventh century, Daphni, Athens, Greece

Christ face, eighth century, Pontianus catacomb, Rome

Christ face, sixth century, silver vase from Homs, Syria

Face on the Shroud

Some early Christ portraits, showing possible influence of the Shroud face. Note the Daphni and Pontianus forehead markings. *(Hirmer Fotoarchiv and Ian Wilson)*

ously unnatural on an otherwise naturalistic-enough work. Another example is a V shape visible between the apparent "eyes" on the Shroud image, and recurring on the Daphni and S. Angelo in Formis portraits, and several others. Altogether, some fifteen Shroud oddities of this kind consistently recur in Byzantine portraits of Christ.

So persistent are these oddities that they have certainly not gone unnoticed by professional art historians. Professor Kurt Weitzmann of Princeton University has remarked of the sixth-century icon portrait from the St. Catherine monastery, Sinai (see page 109):

> . . . the pupils of the eyes are not at the same level; the eyebrow over Christ's left eye is arched higher than over his right . . . one side of the mustache droops at a slightly different angle from the other, while the beard is combed in the opposite direction . . . Many of these subtleties remain attached to this particular type of Christ image and can be seen in later copies, e.g. the mosaic bust in the narthex of Hosios Lukas over the entrance to the *catholicon* . . . Here too the difference in the raising of the eyebrows is most noticeable . . .

For Weitzmann and others, there has been disinclination to consider the Shroud as a possible source of these facial oddities, understandable enough from the point of view of damage to academic reputations if the Shroud were proved a forgery. But such considerations have not deterred Dr. Alan Whanger, professor of psychiatry at Duke University, North Carolina, an enthusiastic spare-time researcher on the Shroud. In 1978, Whanger was so struck by the similarity between the Shroud facial image and that of the Christ portrait on a Byzantine gold solidus minted about the year A.D. 695, that he immediately began experimenting to find the best scientific means of comparing the two images, the one life-size, the other no more than nine millimeters high.

The method he devised was to photograph both the Shroud face and the coin portrait so that each have the same proportions on 35-mm. transparencies, then to project the transparencies from two slide projectors so that they appear superimposed upon one another on the same projection screen. Because such double projection would normally make it difficult to determine which feature belongs to which image, Whanger adds a polaroid filter to each projector, one perpendicular, the other horizontal, and manually rotates a third one. The effect is to enable the areas of congruence between the two images to be observed with ease and precision (color plates 26 and 27).

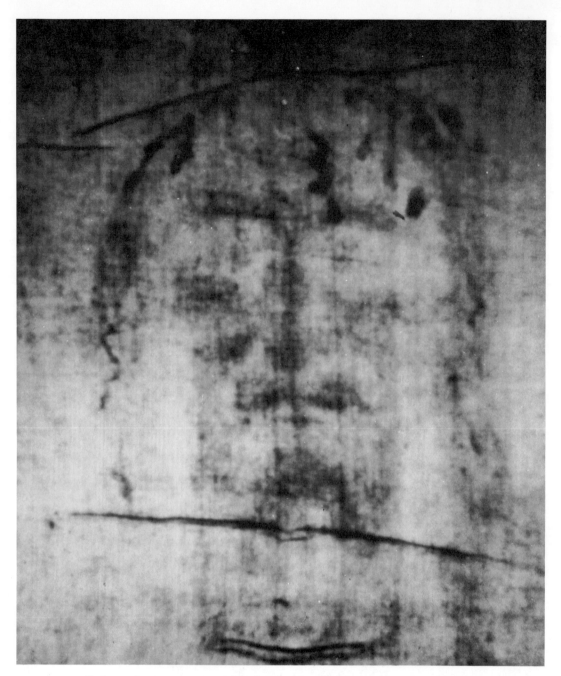

Points of congruency of Shroud image (above) versus early Christ portraits (right), from the research of Dr. Alan Whanger. These numbers show the characteristics of the Shroud face as translated into works of art.

1. Hair parted in the middle
2. Configuration of hair lines on forehead
3. Configuration of hair lines on side
4. Transverse streak across forehead
5. V shape at bridge of nose
6. Heavily accented owlish eyes
7. Raised right eyebrow
8. Configuration of left eyebrow
9. Right eye larger than left, bulges forward
10. Fold under left eye
11. Fold under right eye
12. Left ear incorporating spots
13. Right ear incorporating spots
14. Matter on right cheek
15. Accentuated left cheek
16. Accentuated right cheek

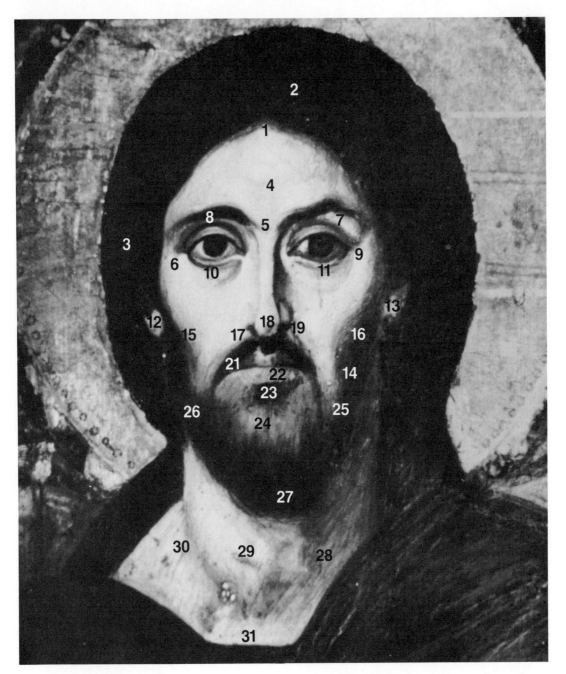

17. Enlarged left nostril
18. Nose tip matches
19. Demarcation of right nostril
20. Accentuated line between nose and upper lip
21. Configuration of mustache
22. Configuration of lips
23. Heavy line under lower lip
24. Hairless area between lower lip and beard
25. Margin of beard on right
26. Margin of beard on left
27. Beard configuration
28. Goiter-like folds of right neck
29. Small fold of neck
30. Jagged lines, left neck
31. Transverse line across throat

(Dr. Alan Whanger, with thanks to Father Damianos, archbishop of St. Catherine's monastery, Sinai; to Father Gregory, head of the Sacred Council, and the other monks of St. Catherine's monastery)

The result throws up so many areas of congruity, including even the matching of Christ's neckline on the coin portrait with a persistent accidental crease on the Shroud, that to Whanger it has seemed self-evident that the Shroud must somehow have served as inspiration for the Byzantine coin. Exploring other Byzantine images, he alighted on the intriguing sixth-century Pantocrator icon from St. Catherine's monastery, Sinai, with the strange features already noted by Professor Weitzmann (see previous page). Following a painstaking study undertaken with his wife, Mary, Whanger claims the identification of no fewer than one hundred and seventy points of congruity between the Shroud image and the sixth-century icon. To them, and to many who have studied their work, it seems irrefutable that artists at least as early as the sixth century somehow had available to them either the Shroud, or a detailed copy of it, seven centuries before, according to Dr. McCrone, the image was devised by some cunning medieval artist.

Importantly, neither the distinctive Shroud-like Christ portraits, nor the facial markings associated with them, are to be found datable before the sixth century. Many pre-sixth-century portraits of Jesus show him as an Apollo-like, beardless youth (see opposite, below). Others, although of a bearded, long-haired type, lack the precision, frontality, uniformity of features, and Vignon facial markings so predominant from the sixth century on. Writing in the fifth century, St. Augustine complained that the portraits of Jesus in his time were "innumerable in concept and design," for the good reason that "We do not know of his external appearance, nor that of his mother." The change came only in the sixth century. From that time on, everyone seemed to know what Jesus looked like, and portraitists, as if by invisible decree, suddenly locked on to the type of representation by which we recognize a picture of Jesus today, complete with the strange facial markings. So what caused them to do so? What, historically, is known to have been the source of inspiration for Byzantine portraits of Christ at that time?

From the point of view of the tradition of the Eastern Orthodox Church, there is absolutely no mystery about this. The universally recognized source of the true likeness of Jesus in art was an apparently miraculously imprinted image of Jesus on cloth, the so-called Image of Edessa, or Mandylion, so highly venerated that a representation of it is to be found in virtually every Orthodox church even to this day. According to a clutch of early writers, this cloth was sent shortly after the death of Jesus to the town of Edessa, present-day Urfa, in eastern Turkey, a location in itself of interest, as it happens to be in the very Anatolian steppe region

21. Christ face, tenth century, church of St. Angelo in Formis, Capua, Italy, showing examples of the strange facial markings that seem to indicate an early awareness of the Shroud.

22. (right) Fourth-century Christ face, from a mosaic pavement found at Hinton St. Mary, Dorset, England, showing beardless likeness common before the sixth century. *(Scala/Art Resource, New York; British Museum)*

23. Shroud face. *(Dr. Alan Whanger)*

24. Face of Christ, sixth century. Encaustic icon from the monastery of St. Catherine, Sinai. 84 × 45.5 cm. *(Dr. Alan Whanger, Courtesy Archbishop Damianos, St. Catherine's monastery, Sinai)*

25. Shroud face and Sinai icon superimposed with the aid of Dr. Alan Whanger's polarized-image overlay technique. By this method, Whanger claims 170 points of congruity between Shroud face and icon, strongly suggesting that the Shroud was the model used by the sixth-century icon painter. *(Dr. Alan Whanger)*

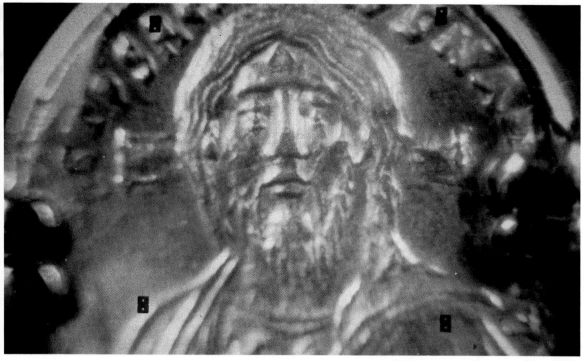

26. Face of Christ, late-seventh century. Gold solidus of the Byzantine emperor Justinian II. *(Dr. Alan Whanger)*

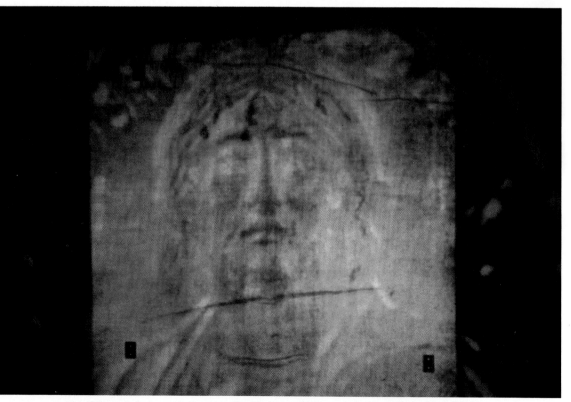

27. Shroud face and face on Justinian solidus superimposed using Dr. Whanger's technique. In this instance, Dr. Whanger claims no fewer than 145 points of congruity, and this from a coin image no more than 9 mm. high. *(Dr. Alan Whanger)*

28. Artist's copy of the Edessa cloth, tenth century, from a fresco in the church of St. John at Sakli, Cappadocia.

29. The equivalent portion of the Shroud when "doubled in four." The Sakli fresco is one of the earliest known depictions of the Edessa cloth and is geographically closest to present-day Urfa, the site of Edessa. (*Lennox Manton and Vernon Miller*)

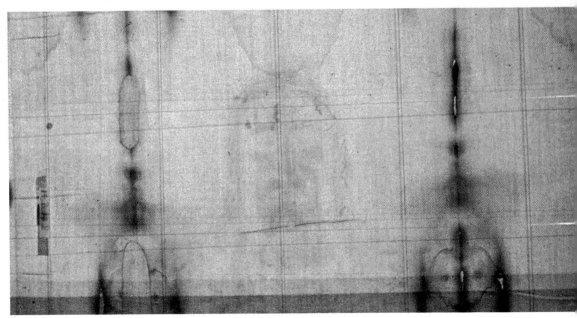

30. The cloth of Edessa being held up by King Abgar, detail from a tenth-century diptych in the collection of St. Catherine's monastery, Sinai. According to Professor Averil Cameron, the small size of the cloth depicted rules out any possibility that the Edessa cloth could have been one and the same as the Shroud. (*Dr. Alan Whanger*)

ѠБРАЗЪ · ГСПДНЬ · NAЦБРVСѢ

31. Icon copy of the Edessa cloth, 17 × 16 inches, early-thirteenth century, preserved in the Cathedral of Laon, France. Note the disembodied appearance of the face and the light-tone "cloth" background. *(Spadem)*

32A. "Holy face" icon in tempera, 39 × 29 cm., preserved in the Church of St. Bartholomew of the Armenians, Genoa. Inscribed "The Holy Mandylion," another name for the cloth of Edessa, it carries scenes of the Edessa cloth's history on its surround. *(Herbert Fried)*

32B. "Holy face" icon formerly kept in the Church of San Silvestro in Capite, Rome, but today reposing, away from public gaze, in the Matilda Chapel of the Vatican. Like the Genoa icon, it is sometimes claimed as the original cloth of Edessa. *(Dante Vacchi)*

33. *Above:* Wooden panel with
strikingly Shroud-like face,
apparently of Christ, discovered ca.
1945 at Templecombe, Somerset,
England, the site of a former
Knights Templar preceptory. Of
late-thirteenth- to early-fourteenth-
century workmanship, the panel
provides an important clue that the
Knights Templar might have once
owned the Shroud. *(Ian Wilson)*

34. *Right:* Burning at the stake of
the Templar Geoffrey de Charny,
together with the Order's Grand
Master, Jacques de Molay, in 1314.
(British Museum)

that Dr. Max Frei's pollen pinpoints as one of the sites of the Shroud's travels. In Edessa, the cloth is said to have been instrumental in the conversion to Christianity of the city's king, Abgar V (A.D. 13–50). Whatever the truth of this, some subsequent persecution seems to have caused the cloth's disappearance, but in the sixth century the cloth was rediscovered, apparently having been sealed for centuries in a niche above the city's gate. The fact of the time of its discovery being precisely that of the dramatic change in Christ portraits can scarcely be coincidental.

Furthermore, from the sixth century on, the cloth is a reliably recorded object, and the contemporary information that can be gleaned is of considerable interest. The early artists' copies show it as a sepia-colored, disembodied image of Jesus' face set on a landscape (as distinct from portrait) -aspect, ivory-colored linen cloth, precisely corresponding to the facial area on the Shroud (color plate 28). Literary descriptions speak of the image as *acheiropoietos* (not made by hand), and refer to its composition as "a moist secretion without colouring or painter's art," "due to sweat, not pigments," and "like drops of blood." In 944 a Byzantine army was sent to remove this cloth from Edessa and take it to Constantinople; it was this which precipitated the prevailing mystery concerning this remarkable object. For when, in 1204, the Fourth Crusade sacked Constantinople, whatever the Image of Edessa was, it disappeared just as completely and inexplicably as the image-bearing *sydoine* described by Robert de Clari.

Inevitably the question that arises is whether the cloth Image of Edessa could have been one and the same as the present-day Shroud. As is unmistakable, if this is the case, its history would neatly fill almost the entire missing portion of that of the Shroud —assuming the latter is genuinely of first-century date.

At first sight, however, there are some powerful objections. For instance, early manuscript accounts of the Edessa Image, almost without exception, describe what was visible on the cloth as only Jesus' face. Direct artists' copies, which because of the relic's holiness occur only from the tenth century on, similarly show only a face. Although manuscript accounts differ in their concepts of how the image was formed, they broadly comprise two traditions:

(i) that Jesus imprinted his likeness on the cloth when he dried his face after baptism;
(ii) that Jesus imprinted his likeness on the cloth when he dried his face after the "bloody sweat" (noted in Luke 22:44) during the agony in Gethsemane.

The universal idea of the Image of Edessa was one of an image of Jesus created while he was alive. And in a direct description of the imperial family studying the Image of Edessa at the time of its reception in Constantinople in A.D. 944, it is quite clear that people of that time had no idea they could be looking at a burial shroud.

While such objections might appear overwhelming, and continue to be so regarded by some historians of Byzantium, their force can be dispelled by one comparatively simple hypothesis: that at the time of its rediscovery in the sixth century, and for at least some while after its reception into Constantinople, the Shroud was folded and mounted in such a way that only the facial area was visible and accessible. On the basis of such a hypothesis, every description of the Image of Edessa during the period in question is compatible with a viewing of the Shroud. Assuming no awareness that it is a gravecloth, the Shroud image's "eyes" appear open and staring, readily suggestive that it was formed while Jesus was alive. Viewed in anything less than the strongest light (a rare commodity in Byzantine churches), the Shroud's "crown of thorns" blood flows are virtually indistinguishable from the rest of the face, hence easily interpretable as from the "bloody sweat" of Gethsemane.

There is much to support such a hypothesis. For instance, the tenth-century official history of the Image of Edessa describes the cloth as mounted on a board and embellished with gold. These features seem corroborated by artists' copies which usually show the cloth stretched taut, as if on a board, and with a multistranded fringe, each strand of which is fastened to one of a row of nails ranged on either side of the cloth. A mounting arrangement of this kind would have been particularly ideal for the conservation of a cloth such as the Shroud, since no nails need have touched the linen itself.

Even more pertinent is early information concerning possible folding. One sixth-century text relating to the Image of Edessa quite explicitly describes it as *tetradiplon*, "doubled in four." A most curious choice of word, according to Cambridge University's Professor Lampe, editor of the *Lexicon of Patristic Greek*, in all literature it occurs only in association with the Image of Edessa, being scarcely, therefore, an idle turn of phrase. The word seems to mean doubled, then redoubled, then doubled again, i.e. doubling three times which has the effect of "doubling in four," producing 4×2 folds. If the Shroud is folded in this manner, the result is unmistakable. The face alone appears, disembodied on a landscape-aspect background, in a manner of the most striking

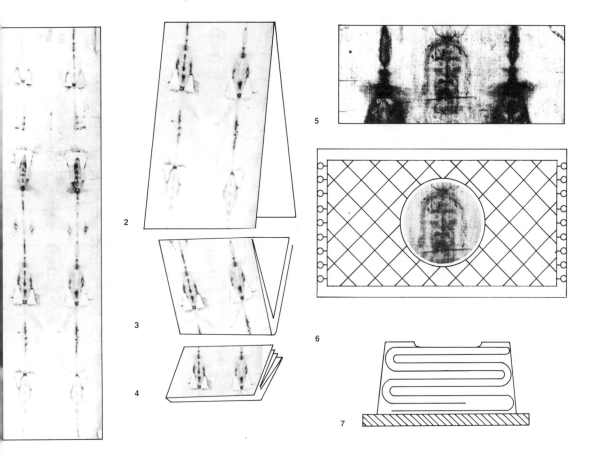

How the Shroud may have been "doubled in four" as the Image of Edessa: 1) The Shroud full length. 2) The Shroud doubled. 3 & 4) Doubled twice again, making 4 × 2 folds. 5) How the Shroud face appears disembodied on a landscape-aspect cloth when "doubled in four." 6) How the Shroud may have appeared as the Image of Edessa, mounted on a board and encased beneath a gold-decorated, trellis-patterned cover. 7) Exaggerated sideways view of the likely "doubled in four" folding arrangement.

similarity to the early artists' copies of the Image of Edessa. The possibility can scarcely be ignored that if the Shroud was indeed preserved in this manner, the Byzantines might have kept it for centuries not realizing it was a shroud (or *the* Shroud), simply because the full-length figure had been sealed away long before their time.

Obviously, it would be considerable support to such a theory if there is direct evidence that at some time while still in the possession of the Byzantines the Image's still hypothetical full-length imprint was suddenly revealed. There indeed seems evidence for this, beginning with sometime in the eleventh century. Without any explanation given, artists at this time begin to show scenes of Jesus' entombment in which, instead of being shown wrapped mummy-style as previously, his body is depicted enveloped in a specifically Shroud-type winding sheet. Several examples of this type feature, for the first time ever, his hands crossed Shroud-style over the loins, a particularly striking example of this being the Hungarian Pray manuscript, reliably dated 1192–95, which, like the Shroud, shows Jesus completely naked. Alongside such artistic evidence, gossip-mongering writers from the twelfth century specifically begin speaking of a full-length body imprint on the Image of Edessa. Ordericus Vitalis, around the year 1130, wrote of it:

> This displayed to those who gazed on it the likeness and proportions of the *body* of the Lord. [Emphasis supplied]

A twelfth-century writer of a Rome codex similarly put into the mouth of Jesus that the cloth he was sending to King Abgar was

> A cloth on which the image not only of my face but *of my whole body* has been divinely transformed. [Emphasis supplied]

As perhaps the most tantalizing clue of all that the full-length figure came to light, from the eleventh century on, the Byzantines began to use in their Good Friday Liturgy beautiful *epitaphioi*, large embroidered cloths explicitly symbolic of Jesus' shroud, complete with a pictorial representation of the full-length body of Jesus laid out in death. In two examples, the finest of which is that of King Uroš Milutin, preserved in the Museum of the Serbian Orthodox Church, Belgrade, the body is represented frontally with the hands crossed in an identical manner to that of the

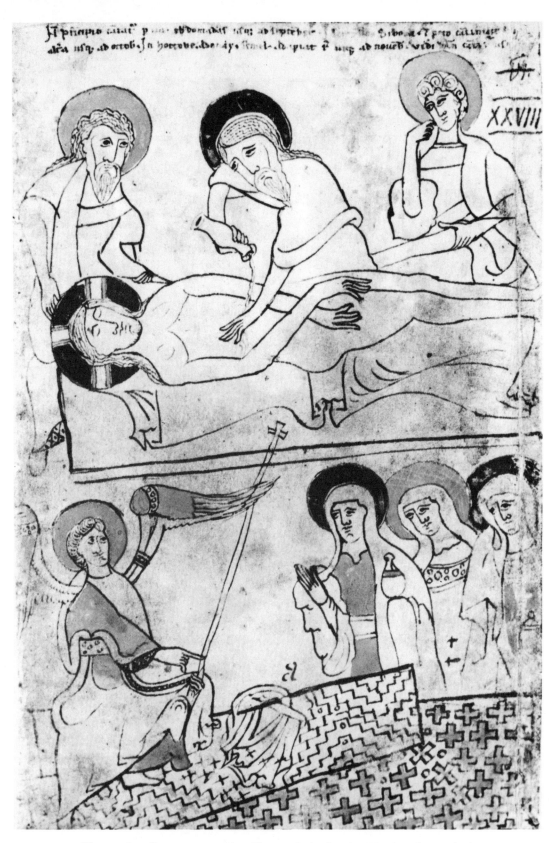

Hungarian Pray manuscript illustration of 1192–95, showing naked, Shroud-like Christ figure, suggesting that the Shroud's full-length image was known by this period. *(Pray mss., Fol. 27v., Budapest)*

Epitaphios, liturgical cloth of king Uroš Milutin, thirteenth century, from the Museum of the Serbian Orthodox Church, Belgrade. *(Ian Wilson)*

Shroud. The date is two generations before the time of Geoffrey
de Charny.

There is, then, at least a reasonable case to be made for the
Shroud's having spent at least half its history in a hitherto unrec-
ognized guise, as the Image of Edessa. If the identification is to be
sustained (and only an eventual first-century radio-carbon date
can provide optimum support), some explanation is of course necessary for what might have happened to the cloth during the
century and a half between its disappearance in 1204 as the Image
of Edessa and its emergence as the Shroud in the 1350s in the
hands of the De Charnys.

There are various possibilities, but according to one Oxford
scholar, Hungarian Dr. Csocsán de Várallja, the most likely person to have whisked the Shroud away during the confusion of the
crusader capture of Constantinople was the Hungarian-born Empress Mary-Margaret, a colorful woman married when she was a
child of ten to the considerably older Emperor Isaac II Angelus.
By 1204, in the course of the vicissitudes preceding the fall of
Byzantium, Isaac had been blinded and suffered two overthrows;
he died during the Crusader capture of the city.

When, after the sack, victorious crusader leader Boniface de
Montferrat took charge of the imperial palace, he found inside the
just-widowed Mary-Margaret, a still attractive woman of twenty-
nine. Boniface proposed to her the same day, they were married
in little over a month, and they subsequently moved to Thessalonica. Here one of Mary-Margaret's few known activities was her
founding of a Church of the Acheiropoietos (i.e. of the Image of
Edessa), a church known today as the Eski Cuma Cami, or Ancient Friday Church. Arguably, she may have done this to house
the Image of Edessa/Shroud brought with her from Constantinople. Perhaps significantly, one of the finest of all known
epitaphioi originated in Thessalonica. Most tantalizing of all,
when, in 1207, Boniface died, Mary-Margaret married yet again,
her new husband being a Nicholas de Saint-Omer, by whom she
had a son William. This William became involved with the Order
of Knights Templar, and whether or not he may have been instrumental in passing the cloth to the Order, what is certain is that
there are good grounds for believing that by the end of the thirteenth century the Templars secretly had the Shroud, or at least
something like it. At this time, all Europe buzzed with rumors
that they were worshiping some form of bearded, reddish-color
male head—sometimes referred to as on a plaque—at secret chapter meetings. Such rumors gave King Philip the Fair of France

the excuse to arrest all Templars and confiscate the wealth of the order in 1307.

Although whatever the original was it was never found, what may well be a copy of it came to light on the site of a former Templar preceptory at Templecombe, in Somerset, England (color plate 33). This is a bearded, Christ-like face painted on a wooden panel, of an unmistakable likeness to the Shroud in its folded form. A further clue lies in the name of one of the highest dignitaries of the Templars, the Master of Normandy, burnt at the stake in 1314 (color plate 34). This was Geoffrey de Charny, a man just one generation before the Geoffrey de Charny of Lirey, who was the first certain (or reasonably certain) owner of the present-day Turin Shroud.

Such, then, is a hypothetical explanation for how the Shroud might not only be a genuine first-century burial cloth, but also have actually played a prominent part in international affairs during the hitherto mysterious years preceding the fourteenth century. The theory, the author's own, has received welcome public support from Robert Drews, professor of classics at Vanderbilt University.

But it has by no means escaped criticism, the most notable opponent being Averil Cameron, professor of classics at King's College, University of London. Professor Cameron has made much of the fact that the earliest known reference to the Image of Edessa, dated around A.D. 400, speaks of it only as a man-made portrait, to her the later "not made by hands" description being thereby dismissable as mere Byzantine fancy. Yet, in arguing this, Professor Cameron has ignored the fact that while in A.D. 400 the whereabouts of the cloth had been lost for centuries, with only the vaguest memories surviving, accounts from the sixth century on derive from the relic's availability at first hand. The latter accounts, which consistently use the "not made by hands" appellation, are therefore arguably the more reliable.

Another point made by Professor Cameron is based on a single early representation of the Edessa Image, one from a tenth-century diptych from the Sinai St. Catherine's monastery, which, she says, clearly shows a small cloth quite different from the Shroud (color plate 30). Yet in arguing this, she has chosen scarcely the most favorable ground. Byzantine art was, and remains, non-naturalistic. Typically, an Orthodox priest once criticized the great Renaissance artist Titian's work with the words: "Your scandalous figures stand quite out from the canvas: they are as bad as a group of statues." Whatever the Edessa Image was, Byzantine "copies" differ markedly one from the other in incidental features such as shape, size, fringe placement, surface decoration, and the like; only by working out a "lowest common denominator" of all copies is some glimmering of the original deducible. But the Sinai icon forcefully conveys a sepia-colored, seemingly disembodied face on a plain linen cloth and matches well the ratio of face to cloth area that would be expected of the Shroud "doubled in four." Although the facial depiction is but a tiny part of the whole icon, Dr. Whanger has identified no fewer than seventy points of congruence with the Shroud face, highly important among these the apparent "neck" exactly corresponding to an ancient Shroud crease line at precisely that point.

Another objection by Professor Cameron has been that it is "beyond belief" that if and when the full-length image of Jesus was discovered on the Edessa Image, the news of this would not have been noised to the world. Such an argument indicates a surprising failure to appreciate the whole spirit of Byzantine Orthodoxy. For the Orthodox, the Body of Christ was and continues to be regarded as so sacred that even today the main rites of the Eucharist are celebrated screened from ordinary public gaze. The Image of Edessa was regarded as too holy for normal human viewing, so that throughout its entire history in the Byzantine world there is no record of a single public exposition, the only possible exception being if it was one and the same as Robert de Clari's *sydoine*. Accordingly, if the whole body of Jesus had been discovered in the Image of Edessa, there is no way in which it would have been deemed prudent to advertise this fact to the common populace. Besides this, the whole tradition of the origins of the Edessa cloth would have needed rewriting. Has Christianity rewritten the Book of Genesis since the discoveries of Charles Darwin?

Professor Drews, for one, has been unconvinced by Professor Averil Cameron's arguments, but there remains one objection, the validity of which is recognized by the author. If the Shroud genuinely spent most of its years up to 1204 "doubled in four," with only the face exposed, this would surely have left some telltale marks on the present-day linen, such as a darkening of the exposed area and vestiges of the original fold marks. Certainly there is no readily perceptible darkening of the facial area, but in fact there is no overwhelming reason why we should expect this. Darkening occurs due to the effect of exposure to light over long periods, and in the case of the Image of Edessa there is no evidence that it received such exposure. A "Liturgical Tractate" quoted by Drews indicates that while in Edessa it was kept in an upright chest with shutters that were opened only for brief intervals during two annual festivals. There were no doubt other times when the shutters were opened for artists to make the close copies that we have noted, but such events, both at Edessa and at Constantinople, would consistently have been in the dim lighting of an ecclesiastical interior, with the most minimal opportunity for darkening to occur.

It is a different situation in respect of the fold marks. Even if the folding arrangement minimized stress, nonetheless one would expect pronounced crease lines after what would have been more than one thousand years in the same position, although the extent to which, with moistening, old linen creases can be smoothed out is quite surprising. In fact, the Shroud's surface, when seen in an appropriate raking light, is literally crisscrossed with creases and fold marks of all kinds, inspiring Dr. John Jackson, in collaboration with photographer Vernon Miller, to make a special study of these as part of the STURP testing program in Turin in 1978. Regrettably, because of the limited time available, it was not possible for Miller to make a truly definitive set of raking-light photographs, but those he took with mere hand-held apparatus nonetheless showed up an intricate tracery of ancient and modern creasing from which John Jackson has been able to make some important deductions.

In a published paper, "Foldmarks as a Historical Record of the Turin Shroud," Jackson claims the pinpointing of at least four of the old Image of Edessa fold marks, with another two reasonably certain and the remainder there by implication. Particularly noteworthy is one fold mark studied by Jackson, that at location C (see photo), which can be traced clearly in the X-ray and ultraviolet photographs, those taken in raking light, and even in the conventional photographs from as early as 1898. Since it occurs precisely one-eighth length from the Shroud's natural halfway fold line, in itself it strongly suggests that the Shroud was genuinely once "doubled in four."

Undeniably, more definitive photographic documentation is required, but certainly there can no longer be claimed to be any absence of fold marks consistent with the Image of Edessa/ Shroud identification hypothesis. If the Shroud is genuinely ancient, its identification with the Image of Edessa remains the most plausible explanation for where and what it was during the centuries before the De Charnys. But it would be quite unwarranted to suggest such a history proved. For that there is still the requirement for the Shroud's fabrication to be positively and irrefutably dated to the first century A.D.

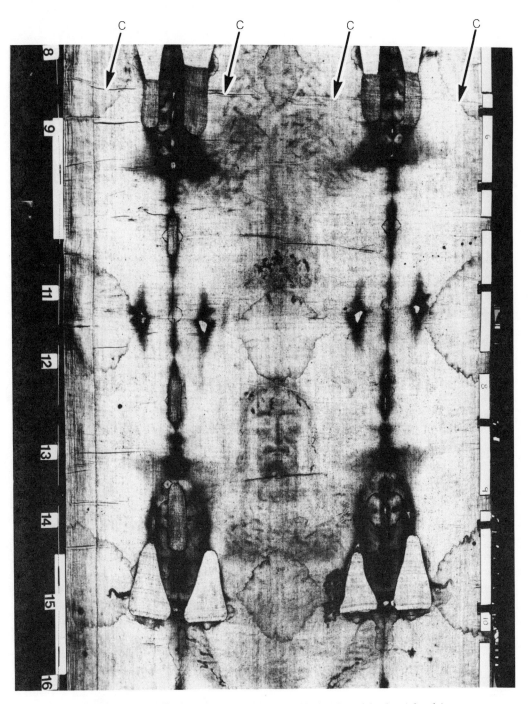

Natural-light photograph of detail of Shroud in black and white showing fold mark visible at Jackson location C. *(Vernon Miller)*

Raking-light photograph of same Shroud detail showing fold marks visible at Jackson locations C and D. *(Shroud Spectrum)*

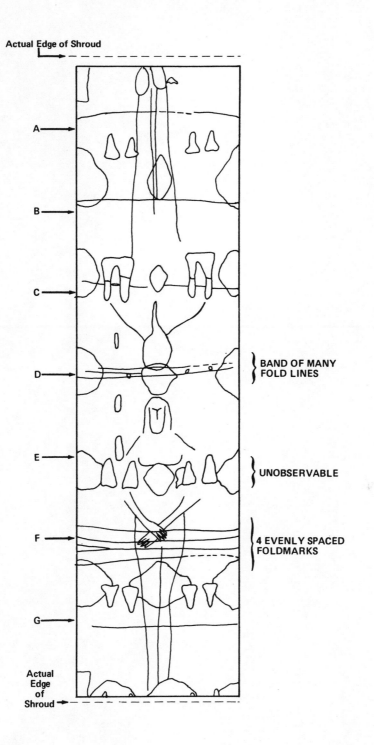

Actual Edge of Shroud

A

B

C

D — } BAND OF MANY FOLD LINES

E — } UNOBSERVABLE

F — } 4 EVENLY SPACED FOLDMARKS

G

Actual Edge of Shroud

Actual locations of "doubled in four" fold marks as suggested by researches of Dr. John Jackson. (*John Jackson, Shroud Spectrum*)

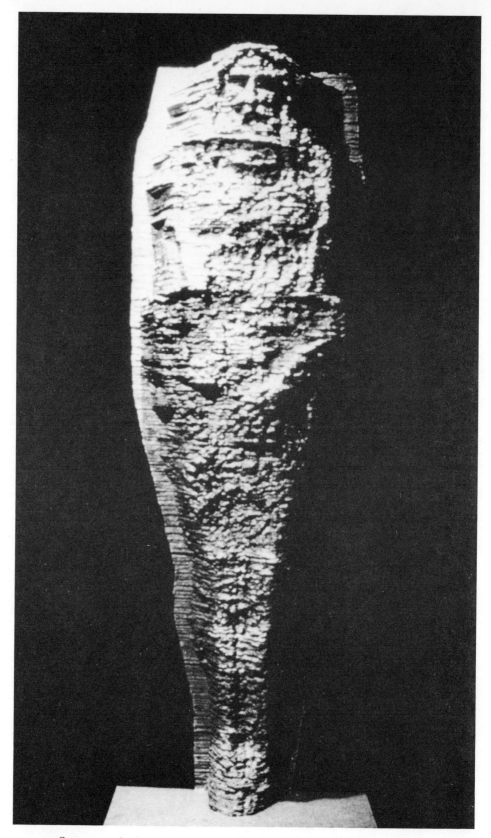

Statue made from VP8 Image Analyzer figures. *(Vernon Miller)*

8

THE SHROUD AND FUTURE TESTING

For the Shroud, genuine or forgery, March 18, 1983, marked the end of an era. That day, there died of bone cancer, at the age of seventy-nine, Umberto II of Savoy, former king of Italy. Although exiled in 1946, Umberto and, before him, his ancestor dukes and duchesses of Savoy had owned the Shroud ever since Duke Louis I and his Cypriote wife Ann de Lusignan acquired it from the aged and childless Margaret de Charny back in 1453. Although in the years following Umberto's exile the Catholic Church, in the person of the archbishop of Turin, had become the Shroud's custodians, in practice most major decisions on the Shroud were usually courteously referred to Umberto at his place of refuge, the Villa Italia at Cascais, in Portugal.

But, as Umberto disclosed in confidence in 1978, in his will he bequeathed the Shroud to Pope John Paul II and his successors, with the proviso that the cloth remain in Turin. For a brief while after Umberto's death, there arose the possibility that his will might be declared invalid, on the grounds that all he owned passed to the Italian state at the time of his exile. But, on October 18, 1983, when Umberto's executors made the formal handover of title to the Shroud to representatives of the Holy See, that possibility failed to transpire. And ironically, despite the years of publicized pressure for "the Church" to allow more testing of the Shroud, it was only at that very recent moment that the Church's effective freedom to respond to that pressure truly began.

But although, apart from a brief showing to Pope John Paul II on April 13, 1980, the Shroud has remained undisturbed since the expositions and testing of autumn 1978, for those actively involved in Shroud research the years that have followed have scarcely been idle. In particular, in the wake of the findings of Drs. Heller and Adler, intensified efforts have been made to try to understand what might have been responsible for the observed cellulose-degradation-type character of the image. Back in 1978, arising from firsthand observations of the Shroud body image's

125

similarity to some of the scorches from the 1532 fire, there was much discussion that the image might have been created by a scorch, perhaps from some searing flash of light at the very moment of Jesus' Resurrection. During the 1970s, an English author, Geoffrey Ashe, had created Shroud-like scorch pictures by applying a heated brass ornament to damp linen. But, as established by the 1978 ultraviolet fluorescence photography, there is a marked qualitative difference between the body image and the scorches. The 1532 fire scorches fluoresce red when irradiated with ultraviolet light, whereas the body images do not.

Another hypothesis, put forward by Dr. Allan Mills of Leicester University, suggests that the image might have been created by some type of electrical discharge between body and cloth, associated perhaps with the earthquake activity described by the Evangelist Matthew as having occurred while Jesus' corpse lay in the tomb. Attempts to simulate some aspects of such a process have been made by Drs. Jackson and Jumper and colleagues in a comprehensive review of the comparative plausibility of every conceivable variety of image-forming process. But although images were produced, as in so many other experiments, these fell far short of the photographic realism of the Shroud. As Jackson and Jumper felt obliged to conclude:

> We have examined a variety of image formation processes in a generic sense and found that . . . no single hypothesis seems to simultaneously explain them all . . .

Nonetheless a quite new and in its own way remarkably revelatory achievement has been made in the course of other studies by Jackson, this time working with Bill Ercoline. As has long been recognized, during whatever image forming process occurred the Shroud must have been draped, as opposed to being flat, over the body it wrapped. This should have caused lateral distortions in the image large enough to exceed natural variations in human anatomy. Ercoline and Jackson determined these, then plotted the actual distortions that would occur with the natural drape of a cloth over a body laid out in the manner indicated on the Shroud. They found good correlation. The effect of this research is to demand that if the Shroud is the work of an artist, he took account of the effects of cloth drape among his many other intricate calculations. Super artist, or supernormal event, consistently these have proved the only two alternatives in the midst of all the many facets of Shroud research.

Recognizing that, despite all their efforts in 1978 and those since, the Shroud still posed many questions that needed further exploration, for Jackson, Jumper, and their colleagues there has seemed only one solution: further testing.

Thanks once again to Father Rinaldi's patient diplomacy, on October 16, 1984, Tom D'Muhala and Dr. John Jackson, as president and vice-president of STURP, together with their Italian scientific counterparts Giovanni Riggi and Professor Luigi Gonella, had more than an hour-long audience with Cardinal Ballestrero of Turin. They presented him with a life-size copy of their latest computer-generated statue of the man of the Shroud, together with a set of proposals for what they hope will be the next round of scientific testing of the Shroud, this time inclusive of radiocarbon dating. The cardinal received them warmly and promised that he would personally pass on their recommendations to the proper church authorities, meaning Pope John Paul II.

At the time of writing, exactly when such new access to the Shroud will be granted remains conjectural. One possibility may be 1988, which would be the Pope's tenth anniversary. This might appear a frustrating delay, but there is much to be gained from the coolest international reappraisal of lessons learned from the STURP work of 1978. Quite aside from radiocarbon dating, there are a variety of Shroud tests and researches either omitted or not altogether satisfactorily dealt with in 1978 which need to be either incorporated or rectified in the event of any new access.

For instance, the unhappy and still imperfectly resolved McCrone versus Heller and Adler conflict might have been avoided if better methods had been used for removing samples of the Shroud's body and blood images. Although sticky tape, still commonly used in criminology, may be considered to have been perfectly adequate for Dr. Max Frei's pollen-gathering purposes, informed scientific opinion suggests it was insufficiently discriminatory for the purposes of isolating the Shroud body and blood images.

In art-gallery scientific laboratories, where analyses are often needed of the paint surface of priceless old masters, smaller-than-the-eye-can-see samples are routinely removed by the point of a scalpel or a needle. Learning of the methods used for the Shroud, Joyce Plesters, the London National Gallery's principal scientific officer, has commented:

> I considered that taking samples from the Shroud by means of sticky tape was a rather crude method . . . It seems to me that with an object like the Shroud, which has a comparatively

rough surface, and which has been lying around for centuries collecting miscellaneous deposits, you would pick up a miscellany of particles, many from the very topmost protruding fibres of the cloth, hence accidental deposits and nothing to do with the original image. It also occurs to me that application of all these lengths of sticky tape to the Shroud has indiscriminately removed a good deal of valuable evidence rather unnecessarily.

Now, mindful of such comments, STURP's recommendations for the future incorporate use of an altogether more precise micromanipulator. Subject to appropriate permission, the intention is also not only to resample body and blood images, but also to make the first-ever analyses of features such as the apparent dirt at the man of the Shroud's feet, the apparent pitch associated with the so-called "poker holes," and much else.

Also to be accorded greater priority and attention in any future testing by STURP would be the method of photographing the Shroud by raking light. Routinely used in art galleries for revealing flaws in the surface of old-master paintings, far better detail of the Shroud's ancient fold marks and other telltale surface weaknesses should be obtainable with due time given to getting illumination quantity and angles absolutely right. STURP has accordingly given this a greater priority in its new recommendations.

But as STURP scientists themselves recognize, there are areas of expertise, outside their own strengths in pure science, which went unrepresented in 1978 and are also vital to fill in weaknesses in understanding of the Shroud. High on this list is textile analysis, no specialist in ancient textiles being among either the Americans or the Europeans who worked on the Shroud in 1978. It was, for instance, regrettable that when one side of the Shroud was unstitched for examination of the underside, no one thought to photograph or in any way document the appearance of the cloth's edges, normally concealed by a blue fabric surround. Examination of the cloth's edges could have provided important new insights not only about the Shroud's original weaving, but how it was displayed in subsequent centuries. Accordingly, textile analysis is one of several hitherto neglected aspects of Shroud inquiry intended to be dealt with by a new research group, ASSIST (Association of Scientists and Scholars International for the Shroud of Turin), who have been specifically formed not to compete with STURP, but to liaise with a variety of international specialists and groups, among these the British Society for the Turin Shroud, with a view to working alongside STURP in any new testing. As in the case of STURP, specific proposals have already been submitted to Turin, ASSIST's program commendably including a replication, by Dr. Aaron Horowitz of the Tel Aviv Institute of Archaeology, of the much criticized pollen analyses by the late Dr. Max Frei.

Given such a new testing, with many international specialists, including ones from the art world, gathered in one place, it may even be worthwhile to include, besides the Shroud, analysis of some arguably related "holy face" icons that have never previously been allowed proper scrutiny. It was suggested in the previous chapter that the Shroud, during the early centuries, may have been one and the same as the Image of Edessa; of some considerable interest, therefore, should be a better understanding of the date and likely provenance of some famous early copies of the Image of Edessa, one preserved in the Chapel of St. Bartholomew of the Armenians, in Genoa, the other in the Matilda Chapel of the Vatican (color plates 32A and 32B). According to Italian Salesian Dr. Luigi Fossati, an X-ray tomogram of the Genoa icon reveals a very Shroud-like underlying image (see overlay). Of equal interest is information from Italian art expert Carlo Bertelli that the Matilda Chapel icon appears to have been painted on a herringbone twill, the identical weave to that of the Shroud (see page 131). Should permission be obtained for these to be examined alongside the Shroud, also highly recommended for simultaneous study would be whatever remains of the so-called "Veronica" cloth, expositions of which once attracted thousands of pilgrims to Rome. Although this seems to have been stolen during a sack of Rome in 1527, a report made eighty years ago indicated that a cloth of some kind is still preserved in the original Veronica reliquary; any relevance or relationship this may have to the Shroud deserves some consideration.

But, without doubt, *the* Shroud test, all too long awaited, is that of independently dating the cloth's linen by the method known as carbon 14. So long has this been awaited that it has given rise to an ingenious though none too orthodox attempt to reach a date by an independent means. In the course of their study of the VP8 three-dimensional images, Drs. Jackson and Jumper thought they could discern small button-like objects, possibly coins, laid over the man of the Shroud's eyelids.

The idea occurred to Chicago theology professor Francis Filas that if these were coins, high-magnification photography might reveal sufficient of the inscriptions for them to be identified and dated. To his astonishment, study of the right eye on a large print of the Enrie negative revealed what seemed to be four letters,

X-ray photograph of Genoa icon, showing the original, more Shroud-like face underlying the present-day image.
(Professor Colette Dufour Bosso)

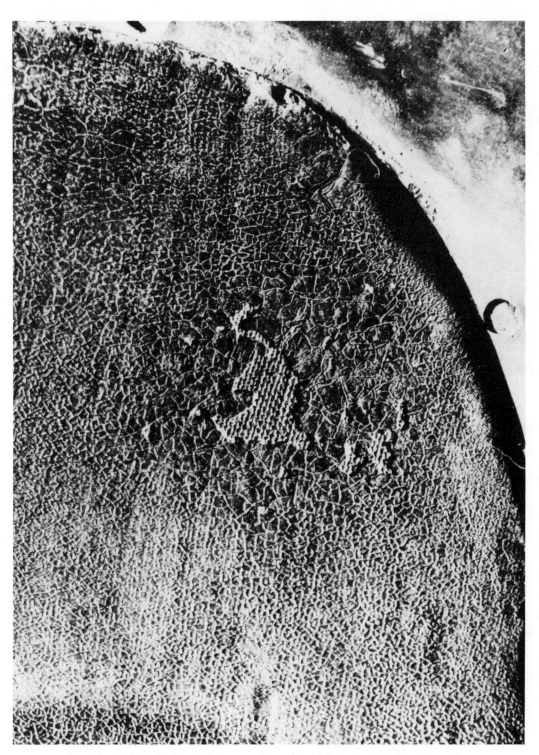

Detail of Matilda Chapel icon, with area of flaked-off paint through which is visible what appears to be herringbone-weave linen. Could this be a cut-off portion of the Shroud? *(Professor Umberto Fasola)*

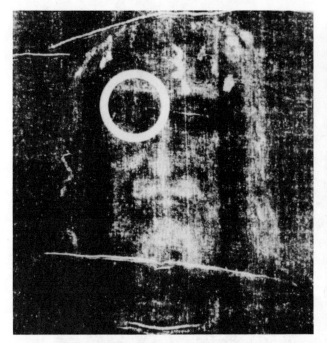

Shroud negative showing possible
location of coin over eye.

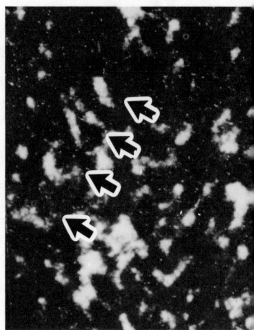

Detail of eye area of Shroud, seeming t
reveal the letters UCAI.

VP8 Image Analyzer detail of UCAI
lettering from Shroud.

Rare example of Pilate lepton with th
inscription TIBERIOU CAISAROS
(Greek transliteration, CAICAPOS). (
Francis Filas and Vernon Miller)

UCAI, arranged in a coin-like curve, surrounding a shape resembling a shepherd's crook (see opposite). As it happens, among the known coins of Jesus' time is a tiny lepton, or mite, of Pontius Pilate, bearing an astrologer's staff *(lituus),* accompanied by the inscription TIBERIOU KAISAROS. Filas surmised that the Shroud UCAI might be the central letters (i.e., TiberioU KAIsaros) with a "C" substituted for the Greek "K," a contention received with considerable skepticism until there came to light two actual examples of Pontius Pilate leptons with precisely this misspelling (see opposite).

Filas subsequently submitted the coin and Shroud image for comparative analysis at Virginia Polytechnic Institute and State University's Spatial Data Analysis Laboratory. Here the director, Robert Haralick, has offered cautious support to Filas' hypothesis while stressing the fundamental problem that science has no way of determining whether what appears as a coin inscription is anything but a random quirk of the Shroud's weave.

In fact, there is little evidence for the Jews ever having used coins to close the eyelids of their dead, besides which pathologist Professor James Cameron has pointed out that such closing of the eyelids would have been quite unnecessary in the case of an individual who had died upright, the weight of the superorbital muscles performing this function automatically. This opinion is not, however, shared by U.S. pathologist Dr. Bucklin of Los Angeles.

So although it would be an immense boost to the case for the Shroud's authenticity if the apparent coin inscription could really be trusted as such, the only arbiter likely to satisfy world opinion of the Shroud's date is the carbon-14 test, the now forty-year-old method of dating ancient organic objects such as wood or linen by gauging the extent to which they have lost their radioactive-carbon-14 content. Because the technology of carbon dating has been available for a long time and has become almost routine in archaeological circles, the Turin ecclesiastical authorities have often been accused of being unnecessarily backward-looking in having failed so far to allow samples of the Shroud to be dated. It has been said that they are frightened of an adverse result and have therefore resorted to every delaying tactic in order to avoid having "the truth" become known. In fact, as has been stressed by Cardinal Ballestrero, the faith of the Church does not rest on the Shroud. Belief in the Shroud's authenticity, or that of any other "holy" relic, is not and never has been required of the Church faithful. In Ballestrero's own words, "The Church has nothing to fear from the truth."

The real reason why the Shroud has so far not been carbon

dated is much more complex and is partly linked to the amount of sample required. Until about five years ago, the test would have demanded the destruction of something of the order of a pocket-handkerchief-sized portion of the Shroud linen, with no guarantee that a second cutting of this size would not be needed if the first test proved inconclusive. However, in very recent years the world's major carbon-dating laboratories have been working on new methods of dating using very much smaller samples, requiring, in the case of linen, a portion no larger than a fingernail. Broadly, two quite separate methods for such work have evolved. One, best represented by the Brookhaven National Laboratory in New York, is essentially no more than a refinement of the old technique. Described as the "proportional counter" method, its minor disadvantage is that in the case of a small sample, up to three months may be required for the actual "counting" of the radiocarbon decay.

The second method, usually known as the accelerator mass spectrometer technique, has been pioneered by England's Oxford University Laboratory for Archaeology and the History of Art and a similar facility at the University of Arizona, Tucson. Involving a three-million-volt accelerator, it counts the actual atoms of radioactive carbon 14, rather than its decay products, and is, inevitably, more expensive. But it has the advantage of being much quicker, it being possible to date a Shroud sample, along with several others, in a matter of a few hours.

Although the Brookhaven method has been available since about 1979, at its very inception it was well known that the mass-spectrometer technique was in the course of development, with fruition expected in the very early eighties. However, development problems, principally with the accelerator, caused delays. It was only in 1983 that the Tucson laboratory announced somewhat qualified success in its dating of a cow's horn purported to have been brought to America by Leif Erikson's Vikings centuries before Columbus. With two runs using eighteen milligrams of scrapings from the inside of the horn, the Tucson equipment produced the following datings:

(1) A.D. 1919 (plus or minus 172 years)
(2) A.D. 2006 (plus or minus 149 years)

A third run, using wood datable from its tree rings to A.D. 1000 produced a reading of A.D. 1036 plus or minus 326 years. Effectively, the success of the cow-horn dating was that it established it, beyond reasonable doubt, to be of modern origin. But somewhat diminishing confidence is the implication of the second reading: that the cow which produced the horn may not yet be born for another twenty years!

As has been pointed out by the British archaeologist Professor Colin Renfrew of Cambridge University, radiocarbon datings are rarely quite as tidy as one would like them, whichever method or laboratory is used. In such circumstances, determining who should carbon-date the Shroud and when is scarcely the easiest task, particularly bearing in mind the wide public debate which will inevitably surround whatever dating result is eventually achieved. Gratifyingly, one man has risen to the challenge the situation presents, STURP scientist Dr. Robert Dinegar of the Los Alamos National Laboratory. Almost uniquely qualified for his task, Dr. Dinegar is both holder of a Columbia University Ph.D in physical chemistry and a theological degree from the College of Santa Fe. Although Dr. Dinegar's work everyday is as a research physical chemist, until his recent retirement Sunday worshipers at the Hill Episcopal Church knew him as their assistant rector. Very quietly and unobtrusively, Dinegar has won interest and confidence in a Shroud dating project on the part of no less than six internationally respected carbon-dating laboratories: in the U.S.A., the Brookhaven National Laboratory, New York; the Nuclear Structure Research Laboratory, University of Rochester; and the Laboratory of Isotope Geochemistry, University of Arizona; in England, the Low Level Measurements Laboratory, Harwell; and the Research Laboratory for Archaeology, Oxford; and in Switzerland, the Physikalisches Institut, University of Bern.

Not only for the benefit of the Shroud but for all similar contentious dating projects, the laboratories have, among themselves, been participating in cross-calibration procedures supervised by Dr. Michael Tite of the British Museum Research Laboratory. These have involved each laboratory "blind" dating identical samples of Egyptian linen of known antiquity (the third millennium B.C.), also fragments of ancient wood, the object being to establish which laboratories are providing the most reliable dating results and which need time for further improvements. Independently, a similar cross calibration, using samples of oxalic acid prepared from modern and fossil carbon, has been instigated by Dr. George Coleman of the Department of Chemistry, Nebraska Wesleyan University. When all the inevitable problems and discrepancies between the laboratories' differing procedures have been ironed out, the way should be open for a dating of Shroud samples so well considered that whatever result is achieved must command respect.

When that time comes, there seems little doubt that the Church authorities, the ultimate decision maker being Pope John Paul II, will allow the requisite amount of Shroud sample to be taken for analysis by an as yet unspecified number of the laboratories named above. Approximately two square centimeters should satisfy each of the six. There is not even need for the slightest impairment of the Shroud's visible appearance. As revealed by the X radiographs taken in 1978, there are substantial portions of original Shroud linen underlying the patches sewn on by the Poor Clare nuns in 1534; suitably unscorched portions of these could be removed without affecting any visible area.

The real unknown quantity is the extent to which *any* result is likely to be sufficiently clear-cut finally to resolve the Shroud issue. Assuming all six laboratories received samples and furnished a consistent fourteenth-century date, that should certainly be decisive enough to cause a massive re-think among those who, in common with this author, support the Shroud's authenticity.

Following the lines of thinking set out in Chapter 5, an interesting detective trail would be set in motion to determine just what manner of centuries-old artist could have fooled so many ostensibly competent modern pathologists, chemists, physicists, and other scientists and scholars.

But almost any other result, even a consistent first-century date, is likely simply to alter the pro-forgery stance, not to destroy it. If the Shroud's linen is proved to be of first-century manufacture, the pro-forgery faction can still argue that the medieval forger simply obtained a genuinely ancient piece of linen for his purpose, because as yet there exists no known means of dating the all too insubstantial body and blood images. If, as is more than likely, various laboratories produce a span of dates, ranging from, say, the second century B.C. to the fourth century A.D., Shroud detractors can offer a choice of arguments. If they accept that the image is of someone genuinely crucified, they can argue that he was simply one of the many thousands of unknown victims of this form of execution prior to Emperor Constantine the Great's ban on the practice in the early-fourth century A.D. Or, if they believe it is a painting, they can argue that it was simply an early-Christian forgery of Christ's shroud.

Obviously the best possible result for those convinced of the Shroud's authenticity would be an unequivocal first-century date for both the linen and its image (a technique possibly helpful for the latter is being developed by Dr. Roderick McNeil of Cambridge Laboratory Technologies, Connecticut) combined with equally unequivocal determination that the body and blood images derive from totally natural/supernatural causes. Even with the most ultrasophisticated modern technologies, expectation of the likely achievement of such a result is almost wildly optimistic, but even then, as stressed by Dr. Jackson and his STURP colleagues, this would be no proof that the Turin Shroud was ever the actual burial wrapping of Christ.

Several modern writers have vastly overstated the case for the Shroud's identification with Jesus. According to Stevenson and Habermas' *Verdict on the Shroud,* the odds are 83 million to one that it could be anyone else. French Jesuit Fr. Paul de Gail, with even more questionable arithmetic, quoted 225 billion to one. Such wild calculations serve to diminish, not enhance, their subject matter's credibility. As wisely and wittily commented by STURP's Dr. Alan Adler:

> The hypothesis "Is this Jesus Christ?" is not experimentally testable. We do not have a laboratory test for Christness.

Ultimately, therefore, whatever result is obtained from any future Shroud testing, it is likely to add to, rather than resolve, the mystery of Turin's so contentious four-meter length of stained, time-damaged linen.

But whatever viewpoint may be adopted, the very existence of the Shroud demands some human response. If the Shroud is one day positively proved to be the work of an artist (and that is well within the capabilities of science), it will nonetheless be a source of wonder how that artist, working centuries ago, could so empathize with the sufferings of Jesus that thousands, if not millions, of intelligent men and women could find meaning in his every daubing.

But even if we cannot prove that it is Jesus, establishment with the best means of science that it is *not inauthentic* can still scarcely be other than awe-inspiring. Without any hyperbole, the close correspondence of the Shroud injuries with those recorded of Jesus, combined with the image's extraordinary singularity, make the likelihood of identification with Jesus at least reasonable. When we then consider that this cloth has survived to our own time, the only age with the technology to begin to understand it, and the very age when material evidence is demanded of everything, we can scarcely do other than ask: Has this been by accident, or could it have been *intended* for our time? Whatever might one day happen to the Shroud fabric, the image that until 1898 lay locked in its stains is now, to all intents and purposes, immortal, reproduced in millions upon millions of copies that have been disseminated to every corner of this planet. Not inappropriate, perhaps, for the only man in history to have promised: "Lo, I am with you always, even to the end of the world . . ."

NOTES AND
BIBLIOGRAPHIES

This book has been conceived as a summary of the latest available information and as a presentation of high-quality Shroud photographs. Readers wishing to explore aspects of the subject in greater detail are therefore recommended to consult the chapter notes and references that follow, coupled with the two bibliographies. The first, general bibliography contains full publishing details of works referred to in an abbreviated form in the notes. The second bibliography provides a full list of all STURP (Shroud of Turin Research Project) scientific papers published to date; several of these will already have been listed in the general bibliography. In case of difficulty tracing specialist Shroud publications, the recent, highly recommended journal *Shroud Spectrum International* is published by the Indiana Center for Shroud Studies, R. 3, Box 557, Nashville, Indiana 47448, and *Sindon* is published by the Centro Internazionale di Sindonologia, Via S. Domenico 28, 10122 Turin, Italy. The address of the Secretary of the British Society for the Turin Shroud is 21 Stanley Gardens, Willesden Green, London NW2 4QH, England.

A comprehensive list of all known Shroud information organizations throughout the world is available from Brother Joseph Marino, O.S.B., St. Louis Priory, 500 S. Mason, St. Louis, Missouri 63141.

CHAPTER NOTES

INTRODUCTION

Because of the scientific testing, 1978 marked a turning point in Shroud studies, and the author's *The Shroud of Turin*, published in that year, provides a fully documented survey of the subject as understood up to that time. Since 1978, there has been an unprecedented flow of books for the general reader, the most prominent being the Reverend David Sox's *The Image on the Shroud*, Father Peter Rinaldi's *When Millions Saw the Shroud*, Kenneth Stevenson and Gary Habermas' *Verdict on the Shroud*, Frank C. Tribbe's *Portrait of Jesus?* Joe Nickell's *Inquest on the Shroud of Turin*, and Dr. John Heller's *Report on the Shroud of Turin*. An excellent color presentation of the subject was provided by Kenneth F. Weaver's "The Mystery of the Shroud," published in *National Geographic* magazine. For an introduction to the skeptical approach, see the articles by Marvin M. Mueller and Steven D. Schafersman in the 1982 *Skeptical Inquirer*.

1: THE MYSTERY OF THE SHROUD

p. 1   *The 1978 exposition.* For a firsthand account of the emotions associated with this event, see Father Peter Rinaldi's *When Millions Saw the Shroud*.

pp. 2–4   *The 1532 fire.* The episode in 1532 in which the Shroud was nearly destroyed is a dramatic tale in its own right; for an excellent account, complete with translation of contemporary documentation, see Dorothy Crispino's "The Report of the Poor Clare Nuns, Chambéry 1534."

pp. 4–10   *Pia's discovery.* For a meticulously researched account, see John Walsh's *The Shroud*, Chapter 2.

p. 5   *The pilgrim's amulet.* This is preserved today in the Musée de Cluny, Paris, and reproduced as one of the plates of the author's *The Shroud of Turin* (photo section between pp. 226 and 227).

pp. 11–13   *The D'Arcis Memorandum.* The original Latin manuscript is in the Paris Bibliothèque Nationale, Collection de Champagne V, 154, folio 138. For a full English translation, see Thurston, "The Holy Shroud and the Verdict of History."

pp. 12–13   *Likeness or representation.* The description of the Shroud as a "likeness or representation" is to be found in a receipt of 6 July 1418: ". . . ouquel est la figure ou representation du Suaire Nostre Seigneur Jesu Christ," published in Chevalier's *Etude Critique*, pièce justificative Q.

p. 13   *The Silent Witness.* The 55-minute documentary film *The Silent Witness* was released for cinema presentation in 1978 and televised on BBC1 in the United Kingdom Thursday, April 12, 1979. It has subsequently been shown in many countries of the world. John Weston's Shroud replica was used in some dramatic sequences in place of the original.

2: THE SHROUD AND THE PATHOLOGIST

pp. 15–16   *Anthropological observations.* Carleton S. Coon's observations on the man of the Shroud derive from an interview with writer Robert K. Wilcox, reported in Wilcox's book *Shroud*. See also the article by William Meacham published in *Current Anthropology*.

pp. 15–16 *Jewish male hairstyling*. See publications by Gressman and Daniel-Rops.

p. 16 *Height in antiquity*. For a chart of the varying statures of skeletons excavated at Giv'at ha-Mivtar, see Haas, p. 45.

p. 16 *Reconstruction of burial attitude*. See article by Ercoline, Jackson, and Downs; also Kenneth Weaver's *National Geographic* article, pp. 748, 749.

p. 17 *Yves Delage*. The original text of Delage's 1902 lecture has been lost but may be reconstructed from his open letter in *Revue Scientifique*. See also the official report in *Comptes rendus hebdomaires des séances de l'Académie des Sciences* 134 (1902), pp. 902–4.

p. 17 *Recent medical findings*. For interpretations of the Shroud by modern medical specialists, see listings under Barbet, Bollone, Bucklin, J. M. Cameron, Judica-Cordiglia, Sava, Willis, and Zugibe, in the bibliography.

pp. 20–26 *Professor James Cameron's observations*. These derive from a lecture he gave to the Manchester Medical Society, England, June 5, 1982.

p. 24 *Dr. Joseph Gambescia*. Dr. Gambescia, a Philadelphia physician, presented his theories on the foot-nailing at a STURP-sponsored Shroud conference held in New London, Connecticut, October 10–11, 1981.

p. 29 *Dr. Michael Baden*. For a summary of his views, see Reginald W. Rhein, article in *Medical World News*, Dec. 22, 1980, pp. 40–50.

3: THE CASE FOR THE SHROUD'S ANTIQUITY

p. 33 *Crucifixion victim*. For a full report on the Giv'at ha-Mivtar crucifixion remains, see Haas, pp. 49–59; also the subsequent articles by Yadin and Møller-Christensen.

p. 34 *Qumran burials*. The information on the Essene burial attitudes derives from Edmund Wilson, *The Scrolls from the Dead Sea*, p. 60.

pp. 34–38 *Textile analysis*. Professor Gilbert Raes's findings were published in an appendix to the Report of the

1973 Turin Commission (see under Raes in the bibliography). For an excellent independent appraisal of the Shroud as an early textile, see the *Shroud Spectrum* article by John Tyrer.

pp. 38–43 *Dr. Max Frei's findings* were first formally presented at the Congresso Internazionale di Sindonologia, Oct. 7–8, 1978, and published in the congress proceedings, *La Sindone e la Scienza*. For the most up-to-date summary in English, see his *Shroud Spectrum* article, also Bulst's "The Pollen Grains . . . ," in a later issue of the same journal. I am indebted to Werner Bulst for the pollen chart published on pages 40–41.

p. 45 *Dr. John Robinson*. See the bibliography.

pp. 45–46 *Washing of the body*. The quotation from the sixteenth-century *Code of Jewish Law* derives from the fourth volume of Solomon Ganfried's work of this title. See also Maurice Lamm's *The Jewish Way in Death and Mourning*. Victor Tunkel's views derive from personal correspondence and from a lecture he gave to the British Society for the Turin Shroud, May 12, 1983.

4: THE 1978 SHROUD TESTING

pp. 47–50 *VP8 Image Analyzer*. Dr. John Jackson's early work with this apparatus is outlined in his paper presented to the 1977 U.S. Conference on the Shroud of Turin. See also his recent paper to the Seattle International Conference on Cybernetics and Society. For independent research on the Shroud image's three-dimensional characteristics, see the publications by Giovanni Tamburelli.

pp. 49–50 *Shroud examination in 1973*. The main source of information on this is the official Commission report *La S. Sindone*, published in the *Rivista Diocesana Torinese*, January 1976. It also incorporates the procedures carried out during a brief earlier examination in 1969. A translation into English has been made for private circulation, courtesy Screenpro Films and the British Society for the Turin Shroud.

pp. 50ff. *Shroud testing 1978*. The information on this testing work has been derived from personal observations in Turin (although I was not admitted to the test room), from discussions with STURP team members, from John Heller's *Report on the Shroud of Turin* (although for factuality this needs to be treated with caution),

and from study of the STURP scientific papers, a
full list of which is published in the second bibliography.

p. 51   *X-radiography.* The main source for this work is Mottern, London, and Morris's "Preliminary Report" in
Materials Evaluation. Duplicates of the X radiographs
have recently become available through the kindness
of Dr. Airth-Kindree of Urbana, Illinois; a fuller,
comprehensive study of these is awaited.

p. 54   *Giovanni Riggi.* A general summary of Riggi's findings is available in Italian in his *Rapporto Sindone.* He
claims to have identified among the Shroud dust evidence of natron, the substance used by ancient
Egyptians to mummify their dead, but British scientists consulted have found difficulty supporting this
particular evaluation.

pp. 56–63   *Photomicrography.* See Pellicori and Evans, "The
Shroud of Turin through the Microscope."

pp. 61–63   *Dr. Walter McCrone.* For scientific papers on the
Shroud, see the bibliography. The quotations from
his research notebook were kindly provided during
personal correspondence.

p. 63   *"Don Quixote" statement.* This was given in the course
of an interview with Chicago *Sun-Times* reporter
Larry Weintraub, published Oct. 24, 1981.

5: THE CASE FOR THE SHROUD IMAGE BEING THE
WORK OF AN ARTIST

p. 65   *Vinland Map.* See McCrone, "Authenticity of Medieval Document Tested by Small-Particle Analysis."

pp. 65–66   *Geoffrey de Charny at Smyrna.* For details of sources,
see note 28, p. 55, of M. Perret's "Essai sur l'histoire
du S. Suaire . . ."

p. 68   *Medieval anatomical studies.* By far the best introduction to medieval attitudes in general is Barbara
Tuchman's prize-winning *A Distant Mirror: The Calamitous 14th Century.* For specific reference to the re-
straints on anatomical studies, and the occasional exceptions, see p. 105 (of U.K. Penguin edition).

p. 68   *Joe Nickell.* See the bibliography.

pp. 68–69   *Noemi Gabrielli.* See her report in *La S. Sindone,* published as supplement to the *Rivista Diocesana Torinese,*
January 1976.

pp. 69–70   *Leonardo da Vinci.* Leonardo's delight in deceptions is
well documented in the account of his life in Giorgio

Vasari's *Le Vite*, first published in 1568. An English-language edition, *Lives of the Artists*, abridged and translated by George Bull, was published by Penguin in 1965.

p. 69   *Madeleine Hours*. See the bibliography.

p. 70   *Maria José*. For Maria José's alleged insight into the Shroud's origins, see Sox, *The Image on the Shroud*.

pp. 70–71   The quotation from Sir Charles Eastlake derives from his *Methods and Materials*, pp. 95, 96.

pp. 71–72   *Representation of a naked Christ*. See W. O. Hassell, ed. *The Holkham Bible Picture Book*, with lively medieval illustrations of Jesus being scourged and crucified.

p. 71   *Chronicon de Melsa*. The relevant passage, ". . . *et hominem nudum coram se stantem prospexit secundum cuius formosam imaginem crucifixum ipsum aptius decoraret*," is to be found in *Chronicon* 3, 35. See P. de Mely, "L'image du Christ"; and Herbert Thurston, "The Holy Shroud as a Scientific Problem," p. 175.

p. 72   *St. Bridget of Sweden*. The reference to Jesus being nailed "where the bone was more solid" (*"quae os solidius erat"*) derives from St. Bridget's *Revelations*, Book 1, Ch. 10.

p. 72   *Canopy for Veronica*. This canopy, or "umbella," would seem to be no longer extant, but a careful record of its appearance was made in the sixteenth century by the Italian Jacopo Grimaldi. The manuscript with his drawings is preserved in the Municipal Library, Florence. See also the article by E. Müntz, although Müntz incorrectly ascribes the canopy to the pontificate of John VII, in the early eighth century.

pp. 72–76   *Easter sepulchre ceremony*. The medieval Easter sepulchre ceremony deserves a complete book in itself. An excellent introduction to this drama is provided in the opening chapter of William H. Forsyth's *The Entombment of Christ*, but for the most exhaustive study see Vol. I of Karl Young's *The Drama of the Mediaeval Church*, esp. pp. 248–397. I am particularly indebted to Dr. Lucas Wüthrich of the Landesmuseum, Zurich, for the opportunity to study and photograph several examples of the Christ figures not on public display.

p. 78   *pitch*. Dr. Ray Rogers' observation of what he thought to be pitch associated with the Shroud poker holes appears in Schwalbe and Rogers' "Physics and Chemistry of the Shroud of Turin," p. 47, note 7.

pp. 78–81   *"boiled in oil."* The quotation from Antoine Lalaing is to be found in Ulysse Chevalier's *Etude critique*, pièce justificative DD.

p. 81   *QED program.* The program featuring an experiment to replicate the Shroud was first screened on BBC1 television in the U.K., Nov. 3, 1982.

6: THE CASE FOR THE SHROUD IMAGE *NOT* BEING THE WORK OF AN ARTIST

p. 85   *Dr. Ray Rogers.* His quoted remarks derive from an Associated Press report from Los Alamos, New Mexico, Oct. 1981.

p. 88   *Dr. McCrone's "I have to confess . . ."* This quotation derives from a letter to the author, Dec. 29, 1981.

p. 88   *X-ray fluorescence analysis.* See Morris, Schwalbe, and London in the bibliography.

pp. 89–101   *Drs. Heller and Adler.* Their formal scientific findings are presented in their articles in *Applied Optics* and the *Journal of the Canadian Society of Forensic Science.* For the general reader, a clear and entertaining account is to be found in Heller's *Report on the Shroud of Turin.* I am also indebted to a lecture given by Dr. Alan Adler to the Chemistry Society, Queen Mary College, University of London, July 20, 1984.

pp. 95–96   *Dr. Gilbert Lavoie.* For his work on the behavior of bloodstains, see Lavoie, Lavoie, Donovan, and Ballas in the bibliography.

p. 95   *Vignon's observations.* See his *The Shroud of Christ*, pp. 28–30.

p. 96   *Prof. Baima Bollone.* See his *Shroud Spectrum* article listed in the bibliography.

p. 96   *Quotation from Dr. Adler.* This derives from his lecture at Queen Mary College, University of London (see note for p. 112).

pp. 99–100   *Volckringer plant images.* See publication by Volckringer listed in the bibliography; also John DeSalvo's "The Image Formation Process . . ." in the bibliography.

pp. 100–1   *Artists' copies of the Shroud.* See the detailed study by Fossati, "Copies of the Holy Shroud," in the bibliography.

7: "NOT MADE BY HUMAN HANDS"—THE SHROUD IN THE EARLIER CENTURIES?

p. 104   *Robert de Clari.* The quotation from crusader Robert de Clari derives from the translation of his work by E. H. McNeal. It should be noted that the original French word *figure* has been substituted for "features," which occurs in McNeal's translation. For justification of this, see Peter M. Dembowski, "Sindon in the Old French Chronicle of Robert de Clari." The original of the De Clari manuscript is no. 487 in the Royal Library, Copenhagen.

pp. 105–20   *Christ portraits in art.* The author has devoted considerable study to this aspect of Shroud studies; detailed arguments are set out in *The Shroud of Turin*, Ch. 12 et seq.

p. 107   *Dr. Kurt Weitzmann.* The quotation from Dr. Weitzmann derives from his definitive work on the Sinai icons, *The Monastery of St. Catherine at Mount Sinai: The Icons*, p. 15.

p. 107   *Dr. Alan Whanger.* Dr. Whanger has a detailed paper of his findings in preparation, but meanwhile a set of transparencies with explanatory notes is available from the Holy Shroud Guild, 294 East 150th Street, Bronx, N.Y. 10451.

pp. 110–13   *Urfa/Edessa.* By far the best authority on the historical background to Edessa, with references to the image (although he does not identify it with the Shroud) is J. B. Segal, *Edessa "The Blessed City."* See also Runciman, "Some Remarks . . ."

p. 111   For a fuller account of the literary descriptions of the Edessa image, see the author's *The Shroud of Turin*, especially Chapters 14 and 16.

pp. 112–14   *"doubled in four."* The sixth-century text referring to the Image of Edessa as *tetradiplon*, "doubled in four," is the *Acta Thaddaei*, available in translation in Alexander Roberts and James Donaldson's *The Ante-Nicene Fathers*, Vol. VIII. Grand Rapids, Mich.: Eerdmans, 1951, p. 558.

p. 114   *Pray manuscript.* See Bercovits. *Illuminated Manuscripts in Hungary*, pl. III.

p. 114   *Manuscript references to full-length figure.* The Ordericus Vitalis quotation is derived from his *Historia ecclesiastica*, Part III, Book IX, p. 8; the Rome codex is

Vatican Library Codex no. 5696, fol. 35, published in P. Savio, *Ricerche storiche.*

p. 117   *Dr. Csocsán de Várallja.* Hungarian-born Dr. Csocsán de Várallja presented his historical theory to the British Society for the Turin Shroud on October 28, 1983; a formal paper is in preparation. Meanwhile a useful summary of his findings appears in Noel Currer-Briggs' *The Holy Grail and the Shroud of Christ,* listed in the bibliography. It should be noted that "Mary-Margaret" is so designated because she was christened Mary in the Orthodox Church, then on being baptized into the Latin Church took the name Margaret. I am particularly grateful to Dr. Csocsán de Várallja for much helpful correspondence.

pp. 117–18   *Knights Templar theory.* The theory that the Shroud was acquired by the Order of Knights Templar is set out in detail in *The Shroud of Turin,* Ch. 19. The theory has been criticized as "brittle" by Professor Malcolm Barber (see bibliography), and undeniably much of the evidence is circumstantial. Professor Barber fails, however, to offer some alternative explanation for the enigmatic and undeniably ancient Templar panel painting found at Templecombe.

p. 118   *Professor Drews's support.* See his "In Search of the Shroud of Turin," esp. Ch. Four. Professor Drews offers different interpretations for some aspects of the Shroud's early history, but on the essential Mandylion-Shroud identification there is full agreement.

pp. 118–19   *Professor Averil Cameron.* Professor Cameron's inaugural lecture "The Sceptic and the Shroud" was delivered at King's College, London, April 29, 1980. Offprints are available from the King's College Department of Classics and History. For a detailed study of the Sinai diptych, see Weitzmann, "The Mandylion and Constantine Porphyrogennetos."

p. 120   *Dr. John Jackson on the fold marks.* See his article "Foldmarks as a Historical Record of the Shroud of Turin," listed in the bibliography.

8: THE SHROUD AND FUTURE TESTING

p. 125   *Death of ex-king Umberto.* For an obituary and assessment of ex-king Umberto's views on the Shroud, see Fr. Peter Rinaldi's "Humbert II of Savoy."

p. 126   *Geoffrey Ashe.* For his personal account of his brass heating experiment, see his "What Sort of Picture?" listed in the bibliography.

p. 126   *Dr. Allan Mills.* For a full explanation of his electrical-discharge theory, see his article "A Corona Discharge Hypothesis . . ." listed in the bibliography.

p. 126   *Jackson and Jumper's image-formation experiments.* See Jackson, Jumper, and Ercoline, "Correlation of image intensity . . ." listed in the bibliography.

pp. 127–28   *Quotation from Dr. Joyce Plesters.* This derives from a letter to the author, July 20, 1982. For an introduction to the latest techniques of scientific analysis of paintings, see her article "Science and works of art," listed under J. Plesters Brommelle in the bibliography.

p. 129   *"holy face" icons.* There is an extensive literature on these icons, including Heaphy's classic *The Likeness of Christ,* but much of this is out of date and unreliable. For the best modern sources, see the works by Bertelli and Fossati.

pp. 129–33   *Fr. Francis Filas.* See the booklet listed in the bibliography. A film-strip with tape-recorded commentary explaining Fr. Filas' findings can be obtained from Cogan Productions, 11134 Youngtown Avenue, Youngtown, Ariz. 85363.

p. 133   *Dr. Robert Haralick.* See his *Analysis of Digital Images* . . . listed in the bibliography.

pp. 133–36   *Radiocarbon dating.* For authoritative descriptions of the very latest small-sample dating techniques, see articles by Chippindale, Gillespie et al., and Taylor et al., listed in the bibliography. I am also deeply indebted to Dr. Robert Dinegar of the Los Alamos National Laboratory, Professor Edward Hall of the Oxford Research Laboratory for Archaeology and the History of Art, and Nick White (formerly of the Oxford Laboratory), for much helpful information and advice.

p. 137   *Identification with Jesus.* For a discussion of the absurd odds which have been quoted concerning the Shroud's being that of Jesus, see Donovan, "The Shroud and the Laws of Probability," also pp. 124–29 of Stevenson and Habermas' *Verdict on the Shroud.* Fr. de Gail's calculations are to be found in the article by Tino Zeuli "Jesus Christ Is the Man of the Shroud."

GENERAL BIBLIOGRAPHY

Ashe, G. "What Sort of Picture?" *Sindon,* 1966, pp. 15–19.

Barber, M. "The Templars and the Turin Shroud," *Catholic Historical Review,* April 1982.

Barbet, P. *A Doctor at Calvary.* New York: P. J. Kennedy, 1953.

Bercovits, I. *Illuminated Manuscripts in Hungary.* Dublin: Irish University Press, 1969.

Bertelli, C. "Storia e vicende dell'imagine Edessena," *Paragone* 217, March 1968.

Bollone, P. Baima; M. Jorio; and A. L. Massaro. "La dimostrazione della presenza di tracce di sangue umano sulla Sindone," *Sindon* 30, 1981, pp. 5–8.

Bollone, P. Baima; and A. L. Massaro. "Identification of the Group of Traces of Human Blood on the Shroud," *Shroud Spectrum* 6, 1983, pp. 3–6.

Bucklin, R. "The Medical Aspects of the Crucifixion of Christ," *Sindon* 7, 1961, pp. 5–11.

Bulst, W. "The Pollen Grains on the Shroud of Turin," *Shroud Spectrum* 10, 1984, pp. 20–28.

Cameron, A. "The Sceptic and the Shroud," inaugural lecture, Department of Classics and History, King's College, London, Apr. 29, 1980.

Cameron, J. M. "A pathologist looks at the Shroud." In P. Jennings, ed. *Face to Face with the Turin Shroud.* Oxford: Mowbray, 1978, pp. 57–59.

Chevalier, U. *Etude critique sur l'origine du S. Suaire de Lirey-Chambéry-Turin.* Paris: A. Picard, 1900.

———. *Le Saint Suaire de Turin, est-il l'original ou une copie?"* Chambéry: Menard, 1899.

———. *Le Saint Suaire de Turin: Histoire d'une relique.* Paris: A. Picard, 1902.

Chippindale, C. "Radiocarbon comes of age at Oxford," *New Scientist,* July 21, 1983, pp. 181–84.

Crispino, D. "The Report of the Poor Clare Nuns, Chambéry, 1534," *Shroud Spectrum International* 2, 1982, pp. 19–27.

Currer-Briggs, N. *The Holy Grail and the Shroud of Christ.* Middlesex: ARA Publications, 1984.

Daniel-Rops, H. *Daily Life in Palestine at the Time of Christ.* London: Weidenfeld, 1962.

De Clari, R. *The Conquest of Constantinople,* trans. from the Old French by E. H. McNeal. New York: Columbia University Press, 1936.

De Gail, P. *Histoire Religieuse du Linceul du Christ.* Paris: Editions France-Empire, 1973.

Delage, Y. "Le linceul de Turin," *Revue Scientifique* 22, 1902, pp. 683–87.

Dembowski, P. M. "Sindon in the Old French Chronicle of Robert de Clari," *Shroud Spectrum International* 2, 1982, pp. 13–18.

De Mely, P. "L'image du Christ," *Mémoires de la Société des Antiquaires de France* 63, 1902.

Desalvo, J. A. "The Image Formation Process of the Shroud of Turin and Its Similarities to Volckringer Patterns," *Shroud Spectrum* 6, 1983, pp. 7–15.

Donovan, V. J. "The Shroud and the laws of probability," *The Catholic Digest.* April 1980, pp. 49–52.

Drews, R. *In Search of the Shroud of Turin.* Totowa, N.J.: Rowman & Allanheld, 1984.

Eastlake, C. *Methods and Materials of Painting of the Great Schools and Masters.* London: Longman, Brown, Green & Longman, 1847; reprinted by Dover, 1960.

Ercoline, W. R.; J. P. Jackson; and R. C. Downs. "Examination of the Turin Shroud for Image Characteristics Associated with Possible Cloth Drape," *Proceedings of the 1982 IEEE International Conference on Cybernetics and Society,* Seattle, Wash., Oct. 28–30, 1982.

Filas, F. *The dating of the Shroud of Turin from coins of Pontius Pilate.* Youngtown, Ariz.: Cogan Productions, 1982.

Forsyth, W. H. *The Entombment of Christ: French Sculpture of the Fifteenth and Sixteenth Centuries.* Cambridge: Harvard University Press, 1970.

Fossati, L. "Was the so-called Acheropita of Edessa the Holy Shroud?" *Shroud Spectrum International* 3, 1982, pp. 19–31.

———. "Copies of the Holy Shroud, Part I," *Shroud Spectrum* 12, 1984, pp. 7–23.

Francez, J. *Un pseudo-linceul du Christ.* Paris: n.p., 1935.

Frei, M. "Il passato della Sindone alla luce della palinologia," *La Sindone e la Scienza,* ed. P. Coero Borga. Turin: Edizione Paoline, 1978, pp. 191–200.

———. "Nine years of palynological studies on the Shroud," *Shroud Spectrum International* 3, 1982, pp. 3–7.

Gansfried, S. *Code of Jewish Law (Kitzur Shulchan Aruch),* trans. H. E. Goldin. New York: Hebrew Publishing Co., 1927.

Gilbert, R.; and M. M. Gilbert. "Ultra-violet visible reflectance and fluorescence spectra of the Shroud of Turin," *Applied Optics* 19, pp. 1930–36.

Gillespie, R.; R. E. M. Hedges; and N. R. White. "The Oxford

Radiocarbon Accelerator Facility, Proceedings of the 11th. International Radiocarbon Conference," *Radiocarbon* 25 (2), pp. 729–37.

Gressman, H. " 'Festschrifte' for K. Budde," appendix to the *Zeitschrift für die alttestamentliche Wissenschaft* 34, 1920, pp. 60–68.

Grimaldi, J. "Opusculum de sacrosancto Veronicae sudario Salvatoris Nostri Jesu Christi," Rome, 1620, *Manuscript Fonds Magliabecchi II*, no. 173, Municipal Library, Florence.

Haas, N. "Anthropological Observations on the Skeletal Remains from Giv'at ha-Mivtar," *Israel Exploration Journal* 20, 1970, pp. 38–59.

Haralick, R. M. *Analysis of Digital Images of the Shroud of Turin.* Spatial Data Analysis Laboratory, Virginia Polytechnic Institute and State University, Blacksburg, Va., 1983.

Hassell, W. O., ed. *The Holkham Bible Picture Book.* London: The Dropmore Press, 1954.

Heaphy, T. *The Likeness of Christ*, ed. W. Baliss. London: S.P.C.K., 1880.

Hedges, R. E. M. "Radiocarbon dating with an accelerator, Review and Preview," *Archaeometry* 23, 1, 1981, pp. 3–18.

Heller, J. H. *Report on the Shroud of Turin.* Boston: Houghton Mifflin, 1983.

————; and A. Adler. "Blood on the Shroud of Turin," *Applied Optics* 19, 1980, pp. 2742–44.

————. "A Chemical Investigation of the Shroud of Turin," *Journal of the Canadian Society of Forensic Science* 14, 3, 1981, pp. 81–103.

Hours, M. *Secrets of the Great Masters.* Paris: Robert Laffont, 1964, and London: Paul Hamlyn, 1964.

————. *Conservation and Scientific Analysis of Painting.* New York: Van Nostrand Reinhold, 1976.

Jackson, J. P. "Foldmarks as a Historical Record of the Turin Shroud," *Shroud Spectrum* 11, 1984, pp. 6–29.

————; E. J. Jumper; and W. Ercoline. "The Three Dimensional Characteristics of the Shroud Image," *Proceedings of the 1982 IEEE International Conference on Cybernetics and Society*, Seattle, Oct. 28–30, 1982.

————. "Correlation of image intensity on the Turin Shroud with the 3-D structure of a human body shape," *Applied Optics* 23, July 1984, pp. 2244–70.

Jackson, J. P.; E. J. Jumper; W. Mottern; and K. Stevenson. "The three-dimensional image of Jesus' burial cloth," *Proceedings of the 1977 U.S. Conference of Research on the Shroud of Turin*, ed. K. Stevenson. New York: Holy Shroud Guild, 1977, pp. 74–94.

Jumper, E. J.; A. D. Adler; J. P. Jackson; S. F. Pellicori; J. H. Heller; and J. Druzik. "A Comprehensive Examination of the Various Stains and Images on the Shroud of Turin," *ACS Advances in Chemistry No. 205 Archaeological Chemistry III*, ed. Joseph B. Lambert. American Chemical Society, 1984, pp. 447–76.

Judica-Cordiglia, G. *La Sindone*. Padua: Lice, 1961.

Lamm, M. *The Jewish Way in Death and Mourning*. New York: Jonathan David, 1969.

Lavoie, B. B.; G. R. Lavoie; D. Klutstein; and J. Regan. "In accordance with Jewish burial custom the body of Jesus was not washed," *Sindon* 30, 1981.

Lavoie, G. R.; B. B. Lavoie; V. J. Donovan; and J. S. Ballas. "Blood on the Shroud of Turin: Part II," *Shroud Spectrum* 8, 1983, pp. 2–10.

McCrone, W. C. "Authenticity of Medieval Document Tested by Small-Particle Analysis," *Analytical Chemistry* 48, 8, 1976, pp. 676–79A.

———. "Light-Microscopical Study of the Turin 'Shroud' " III, *The Microscope* 29, 1981, pp. 19–38.

———; and C. Skirius. "Light-Microscopical Study of the Turin 'Shroud' " I & II, *The Microscope* 28, 1980, pp. 1–13.

Meacham, W. "The Authentication of the Turin Shroud: An Issue in Archaeological Epistemology," *Current Anthropology* 24, 3, June 1983, pp. 283–312.

Miller, V. D.; and S. F. Pellicori. "Ultraviolet Fluorescence Photography of the Shroud of Turin," *Journal of Biological Photography* 49, 3, 1981, pp. 71–85.

Mills, A. A. "A Corona Discharge Hypothesis for the Mechanism of Image Formation on the Turin Shroud," *General Report and Proceedings of the British Society for the Turin Shroud*, 1981, pp. 14–21.

Møller-Christensen, V. "Skeletal Remains from Giv'at ha-Mivtar," *Israel Exploration Journal* 26, 1976, pp. 35–38.

Morris, R. A.; L. S. Schwalbe; and R. J. London. "X-ray Fluorescence Investigation of the Shroud of Turin," *X-Ray Spectrometry* 9, 2, 1980, pp. 40–47.

Mottern, R. W.; R. J. London; and R. A. Morris. "Radiographic Examination of the Shroud of Turin: A Preliminary Report," *Materials Evaluation* 38, 12, 1979, pp. 39–44.

Mueller, M. M. "The Shroud of Turin: A critical appraisal," *The Skeptical Inquirer* 6, 3, pp. 15–34.

Müntz, E. "Une broderie inédite exécutée pour le Pape Jean

VII," *Revue de l'art chrétien*, 1900, pp. 18–21.

Nickell, J. "The Turin Shroud: Fake? Fact? Photograph?" *Popular Photography* 85, 5, 1979, pp. 97–99, 146, 147.

———. "New Evidence: The Shroud of Turin Is a Forgery," *Free Inquiry* 1, 3, 1981, pp. 28–30.

———. *Inquest on the Shroud of Turin*. Buffalo, N.Y.: Prometheus Books, 1983.

Pellicori, S. F. "Spectral Properties of the Shroud of Turin," *Applied Optics* 19, 12, 1980, pp. 1913–20.

———; and M. S. Evans. "The Shroud of Turin Through the Microscope," *Archaeology*, Jan.–Feb. 1981, pp. 32–43.

Perret, M. "Essai sur l'histoire du S. Suaire du XIVe au XVIe siècle," *Mémoires de l'Académie des Sciences, Belles Lettres et Arts de Savoie* IV, 1960, pp. 49–121.

Plesters Brommelle, J.; and N. S. Plesters Brommelle. "Science and works of art," *Nature* 250, Aug. 30, 1974.

Raes, G. "Rapport d'Analise," *La S. Sindone* supplement to *Rivista Diocesana Torinese*, Turin, Jan. 1976, pp. 79–83.

Rhein, R. W., Jr. "The Shroud of Turin," *Medical World News*, Dec. 22, 1980, pp. 40–50.

Riggi, G. "The Dusts of the Holy Shroud of Turin" and "Electronic Scanning Microscopy and Microanalysis of Dust Taken from Burial Fabrics of Egyptian Mummies, in Relation to Dust Taken from the Shroud of Turin," papers presented at STURP conference, New London, Conn., Oct. 9, 1981.

———. *Rapporto Sindone, 1978–82*. Turin: Il piccolo editore, 1982.

Rinaldi, P. *When Millions Saw the Shroud*. New York: Don Bosco, 1979.

———. "Humbert II of Savoy 1904–1983," *Shroud Spectrum* 7, 1983, pp. 3–5.

Robinson, J. A. T. "The Shroud and the New Testament." In P. Jennings, ed. *Face to Face with the Turin Shroud*. Oxford: Mowbray, 1978, pp. 69–80.

Runciman, S. "Some Remarks on the Image of Edessa," *Cambridge Historical Journal* 111, 1931, pp. 238 ff.

Sava, A. F. "The wounds of Christ," *Catholic Biblical Quarterly* 16, 1957, pp. 438–43.

Savio, P. *Ricerche storiche sulla Santa Sindone*. Turin: n.p., 1957.

Schafersman, S. D. "Science, the public and the Shroud of Turin," *The Skeptical Inquirer* 6, 3, 1982, pp. 37–56.

Schwalbe, L.; and R. N. Rogers. "Physics and Chemistry of the Shroud of Turin: A Summary of the 1978 Investigation," *Analytica Chimica Acta* 135, 1982, pp. 3–49.

Segal, J. *Edessa "The Blessed City."* Oxford: Oxford University Press, 1970.

Sox, D. *The Image on the Shroud: Is the Turin Shroud a Forgery?* London: Unwin, 1981.

Stevenson, K.; and G. Habermas. *Verdict on the Shroud.* Ann Arbor, Mich.: Servant, 1981.

Strong, L. "Extensive damage to Mummy H7386 by Demestid Beetle," *Proceedings of the Bristol Naturalists Society* 40, 1981, pp. 27–29.

Tamburelli, G. "La Sindone dopo l'eborazione tridimensionale," *L'Osservatore Romano,* Nov. 7, 1979.

———. "Reading the Shroud with the aid of the computer," *Shroud Spectrum International* 2, 1982, pp. 3–11.

Taylor, R. E.; D. J. Donahue; T. H. Zabel; P. E. Damon; and A. J. T. Jull. "Radiocarbon Dating by Particle Accelerators: An Archaeological Perspective," *ACS Advances in Chemistry no. 205, Archaeological Chemistry III,* ed. Joseph B. Lambert, American Chemical Society, 1984.

Thurston, H. "The Holy Shroud as a Scientific Problem," *The Month* 101, 1903, pp. 162–78.

———. "The Holy Shroud and the Verdict of History," *The Month* 101, 1903, pp. 17–29.

Tribbe, F. C. *Portrait of Jesus?* New York: Stein & Day, 1983.

Tuchman, B., *A Distant Mirror: The Calamitous 14th Century.* New York: Alfred A. Knopf., 1978.

Tyrer, J. "Looking at the Turin Shroud as a Textile," *Shroud Spectrum International* 6, 1983, pp. 35–45.

Vignon, P. *The Shroud of Christ.* London: Constable, 1902.

———. *Le Saint Suaire de Turin devant la science, l'archéologie, l'histoire, l'iconographie, la logique.* Paris: Masson, 1939.

Volckringer, J. *Le problème des empreintes devant la science.* Paris: Libraire du Carmel, 1942; republished 1982.

Walsh, J. *The Shroud.* New York: Random House, 1963.

Weaver, K. "The Mystery of the Shroud," *National Geographic* 157, 1980, pp. 730–53.

Weitzmann, K. "The Mandylion and Constantine Porphyrogennetos," *Cahiers Archéologiques* XI, 1960, pp. 165–84.

———. *The Monastery of St. Catherine at Mount Sinai: The Icons,* Vol. I. Princeton, N.J.: Princeton University Press, 1976.

Whanger, A. "Polarized Image Overlay Technique: A New Image Comparison Method and Its Applications," *Applied Optics* 24, no. 16, March 15, 1985, pp. 766–72.

Wilcox, R. K. *Shroud.* New York: Macmillan, 1977.

Willis, A. D. "Did He Die on the Cross?" *Ampleforth Journal* 74, 1969, pp. 27–39.

Wilson, E. *The Scrolls from the Dead Sea.* London: W. H. Allen, 1955.

Wilson, I. *The Shroud of Turin*. Garden City, N.Y.: Doubleday, 1978.

Yadin, Y. "Epigraphy and Crucifixion," *Israel Exploration Journal* 23, 1973, pp. 18–20.

Young, K. *The Drama of the Mediaeval Church*. Oxford: Clarendon Press, 1933.

Zantiflet, C. *Chronicon*, in *Vetetum scriptorum et monumentorum historicorum amplissima collectis*. T.V., col. 254.

Zeuli, T. "Jesus Christ Is the Man of the Shroud," *Shroud Spectrum* 10, 1984, pp. 29–33.

Zugibe, F. T. *The Cross and the Shroud*. New York: Angelus Books, 1982.

BIBLIOGRAPHY OF STURP (SHROUD OF TURIN RESEARCH PROJECT) PUBLISHED SCIENTIFIC PAPERS

Before 1978 testing
Proceedings of the 1977 United States Conference of Research on the Shroud of Turin, March 23–24, 1977, Albuquerque, New Mexico, Holy Shroud Guild, 1977

Accetta, J. "Infrared Thermography with Applications to the Shroud of Turin."

———. "X-Ray Fluorescence Analysis with Application to the Shroud of Turin."

Devan, D. "Photography of the Turin Shroud for Use in Image Analysis Experiments."

———; J. Jackson; and E. Jumper. "Computer Related Investigations of the Holy Shroud."

German, D. "An Electronic Technique for Constructing an Accurate Three-Dimensional Shroud Image."

Jackson, J. "Color Analysis of the Turin Shroud: A Preliminary Study."

———. "A Problem of Resolution Posed by the Existence of a Three-Dimensional Image on the Shroud."

———; E. Jumper; W. Mottern; and K. Stevenson. "The Three-Dimensional Image on Jesus' Burial Cloth."

Janney, D. "Computer-Aided Image Enhancement and Analysis."

Jumper, E. "Considerations of Molecular Diffusion and Radiation as an Image Formation Process on the Shroud."

LaRue, R. "Tonal Distortions in Shroud Image Photographs."

Lorre, J.; and D. Lynn. "Digital Enhancement of Images of the Shroud of Turin."

Rogers, R. "Chemical Considerations Concerning the Shroud of Turin."

La Sindone e La Scienza, Atti Del Il Congresso Internazionale di Sindonologia 1978. Turin: Edizioni Paoline, 1979.

Bucklin, Robert. "A Pathologist Looks at the Shroud of Turin."

Jackson, J. P.; and E. J. Jumper. "Space Science and the Holy Shroud."

After 1978 testing

Accetta, J. S.; and J. S. Baumgart. "Infrared Reflectance Spectroscopy and Thermographic Investigations of the Shroud of Turin," *Applied Optics,* Vol. 19, no. 12, pp. 1921–29, June 15, 1980.

Avis, C.; D. Lynn; J. Lorre; S. Lavoie; J. Clark; E. Armstrong; and J. Addington. "Image Processing of the Shroud of Turin," *IEEE 1982 Proceedings of the International Conference on Cybernetics and Society,* #0360-8913/82/0000-0554, pp. 554–58, October 1982.

Bucklin, Robert. "The Shroud of Turin: A Pathologist's Viewpoint," *Legal Medicine Annual,* 1982.

————. "The Shroud of Turin: Viewpoint of a Forensic Pathologist," *Shroud Spectrum International,* Vol. 1, no. 5, pp. 2–10, December 1982.

Devan, D. "Quantitative Photography of the Shroud of Turin," *IEEE 1982 Proceedings of the International Conference on Cybernetics and Society,* #0360-8913/82/0000-0548, pp. 548–53, October 1982.

Dinegar, Robert H. "The 1978 Scientific Study of the Shroud of Turin," *Shroud Spectrum International,* Vol. 1, no. 4, pp. 2–12, September 1982.

Ercoline, W. R.; R. C. Downs, Jr.; and J. P. Jackson. "Examination of the Turin Shroud for Image Distortions," *IEEE 1982 Proceedings of the International Conference on Cybernetics and Society,* #0360-8913/82/0000-0576, pp. 576–79, October 1982.

Gilbert, R., Jr.; and Marion M. Gilbert. "Ultraviolet–Visible Reflectance and Fluorescence Spectra of the Shroud of Turin," *Applied Optics,* Vol. 19, no. 12, pp. 1930–36, June 15, 1980.

Heller, J. H.; and A. D. Adler. "Blood on the Shroud of Turin," *Applied Optics,* Vol. 19, no. 16, pp. 2742–44, Aug. 14, 1980.

————. "A Chemical Investigation of the Shroud of Turin," *Can. Soc. Forens. Sci. J.,* Vol. 14, no. 3, pp. 81–103, 1981.

Jackson, J. P. "Foldmarks as a Historical Record of the Turin Shroud," *Shroud Spectrum International,* No. 11, pp. 6–29, June 1984.

————; and Eric J. Jumper. "The Three Dimensional Images on the Holy Shroud," *Sindon,* October 1977.

————; and Ercoline, W. R. "Three Dimensional Characteristic of the Shroud Image," *IEEE 1982 Proceedings of the International Conference on Cybernetics and Society,* #0360-8913/82/0000-0559, pp. 559–75, October 1982.

———. "Correlation of Image Intensity of the Turin Shroud with the 3-D Structure of a Human Body Shape," *Applied Optics*, Vol. 23, no. 14, pp. 2244–70, July 15, 1984.

Jumper, E. J. "An Overview of the Testing Performed by the Shroud of Turin Research Project with a Summary of Results," *IEEE 1982 Proceedings of the International Conference on Cybernetics and Society*, #0360-8913/82/0000-0535, pp. 535–37, October 1982.

———; A. D. Adler; J. P. Jackson; S. F. Pellicori; J. H. Heller; and J. R. Druzik. "A Comprehensive Examination of Various Stains and Images on the Shroud of Turin," *ACS Advances in Chemistry, No. 205, Archaeological Chemistry III*, Joseph B. Lambert, ed., pp. 447–76, 1984.

Jumper, E. J.; and R. W. Mottern. "Scientific Investigation of the Shroud of Turin," *Applied Optics*, Vol. 19, no. 12, June 15, 1980, pp. 1909–12.

Miller, V.; and D. Lynn. "De Lijkwade Van Turijn," *Natuur en Techniek*, February 1981, pp. 102–25.

Miller, V. D.; and S. F. Pellicori. "Ultraviolet Fluorescence Photography of the Shroud of Turin," *Journal of Biological Photography*, Vol. 49, no. 3, July 1981, pp. 71–85.

Morris, R. A.; L. A. Schwalbe; and J. R. London. "X-Ray Fluorescence Investigation of the Shroud of Turin," *X-Ray Spectrometry*, Vol. 9, no. 2, pp. 40–47, 1980.

Mottern, R. W.; R. J. London; and R. A. Morris. "Radiographic Examination of the Shroud of Turin—a Preliminary Report," *Materials Evaluation*, Vol. 38, no. 12, 1979, pp. 39–44.

Pellicori, S. F. "Spectral Properties of the Shroud of Turin," *Applied Optics*, Vol. 19, no. 12, June 15, 1980, pp. 1913–20.

———. "Spectrochemical Results of the 1978 Investigation," *Sindon*, 1981.

———; and R. A. Chandos. "Portable Unit Permits UV/VIS Study of the Shroud," *Industrial Research and Development*, February 1981.

Pellicori, S.; and M. Evans. "The Shroud of Turin Through the Microscope," *Archaeology*, Jan.–Feb. 1981, pp. 35–43.

Riggi, G. *Rapporto Sindone 1978–82*. Il Piccolo Editore, Turin: 1980.

Schwalbe, L. A.; and R. N. Rogers. "Physics and Chemistry of the Shroud of Turin," *Analytica Chimica Acta* 135, 1982, pp. 3–49.

Schwortz, B. M. "Mapping of Research Test-Point Areas on the Shroud of Turin," *IEEE 1982 Proceedings of the International Conference on Cybernetics and Society*, #0360-8913/82/0000-0538, pp. 538–47, October 1982.

INDEX

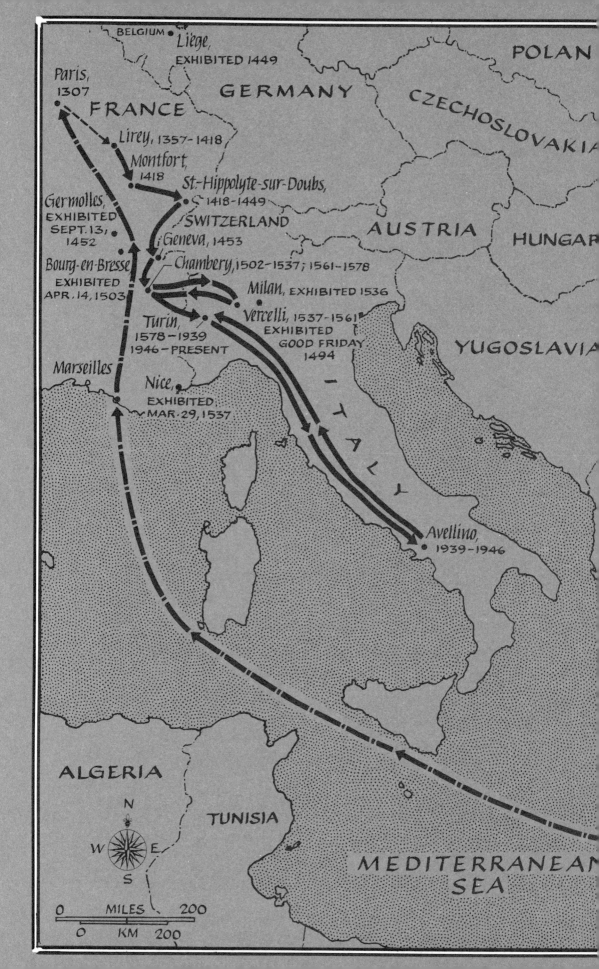

BELGIUM • Liège,
EXHIBITED 1449

POLAN

GERMANY

CZECHOSLOVAKIA

Paris,
1307
FRANCE

Lirey, 1357–1418

Montfort,
1418
St.-Hippolyte-sur-Doubs,
1418–1449

Germolles,
EXHIBITED
SEPT. 13,
1452

SWITZERLAND

AUSTRIA

HUNGAR

Geneva, 1453

Bourg-en-Bresse
EXHIBITED
APR. 14, 1503

Chambery, 1502–1537; 1561–1578

Milan, EXHIBITED 1536

YUGOSLAVIA

Turin,
1578–1939
1946–PRESENT

Vercelli, 1537–1561
EXHIBITED
GOOD FRIDAY
1494

I T A L Y

Marseilles

Nice,
EXHIBITED
MAR. 29, 1537

Avellino,
1939–1946

ALGERIA

N

TUNISIA

W   E

S

MEDITERRANEAN
SEA

0   MILES   200

0   KM   200